Our
Land

The Canadian Issues Series

James Lorimer & Company has developed this series of original paperbacks to offer informed, up-to-date, critical introductions to key issues facing Canadians. Books are written specifically for the series by authors commissioned by the publisher on the basis of their expertise in a subject area and their ability to write for a general audience.

The 4'' x 7'' paperback format and cover design for the series offer attractive books at the lowest possible price. Special library hard-bound editions are also available. New titles are added to the series every spring and fall: watch for them in your local bookstore.

DONALD PURICH

Our
Land

Native Rights in Canada

James Lorimer & Company, Publishers
Toronto 1986

Cover design: Brant Cowie
Cover photograph: René Fumoleau

Canadian Cataloguing in Publication Data
  Purich, Donald J., 1947-
    Our land: native rights in Canada

  (Canadian issue series)
  Bibliography: p.
  Includes index.

  ISBN 0-88862-975-3 (bound). - ISBN 0-88862-974-
  5 (pbk.)

  1. Indians of North America - Canada - Government relations. 2. Indians, Treatment of - Canada
  - History. 3. Indians of North America - Canada
  - History. I. Title. II. Series: Canadian issues
  series (Toronto, Ont.)

  E92.P87 1986   323.1'197'071   C86-
  094499-9

James Lorimer & Company, Publishers
Egerton Ryerson Memorial Building
35 Britain Street
Toronto, Ontario M5A 1R7

Printed and bound in Canada
6 5 3   88 89 90

Contents

To
Karen

Acknowledgements

A number of people and institutions were most helpful to me in the preparation of this book. The Native Law Centre library at the University of Saskatchewan was a most valuable resource. The library's news clipping service and collection of back issues of native newspapers was particularly useful. Librarian Linda Fritz was especially helpful in finding materials and answering many questions about government reports and materials.

Professor Richard Bartlett, at the College of Law, University of Saskatchewan, was kind enough to read a draft of the manuscript and made many useful suggestions for improvement. Professor Bartlett also answered many questions for me during the writing of the book.

My colleagues Ruth Thompson and Norman Zlotkin, at the Native Law Centre, also were helpful. Ruth answered many of my questions on indigenous people and international law; while Norman provided me with information on native people and the Constitution.

Other colleagues at the university were also helpful: Professors F. Laurie Barron, of the Native Studies Department, Dale Miquelon (formerly of the History

Department) and Jim Miller of the History Department were able to provide me with essential information on a number of subjects. Professor Howard McConnell from the College of Law answered a number of questions dealing with constitutional matters. Johanne Cadieux, archivist at the university's Diefenbaker Centre, found a number of relevant Diefenbaker speeches for me. Brenda Shular from the Administrative Systems and Programming Department helped with several computer matters relating to preparing the manuscript for publication.

Ted Mumford, trade editor at James Lorimer and Company, made a number of excellent editorial suggestions for improving the manuscript.

While many people provided me with assistance the judgements and opinions are entirely my own.

1
The First Peoples

Several men scale a tree. At the top they drive a stone wedge downward to start a split to the bottom, to produce a plank for a house they will soon be building in a nearby village. They slip a long pole into the incision made by the wedge; the weight of the pole and the tree's swaying in the wind will cause the split to work its way down to the bottom of the tree. The men will return to the tree later to collect the first plank, and to repeat the process to produce another.

Back at the village, other men using stakes and measured ropes are surveying a site for the new house. When completed it will be approximately 30 feet wide and 100 feet long. The house will have a sloping roof, with the boards curved lengthwise in the centre, overlapping to form a water-tight roof. The house will have a polished wood floor and a central fireplace.

The day the house is to be raised, a team of men using pivots, levers and guide poles will erect the huge beams necessary to hold the house together. Storage ledges, made of earth banks, will be built along the outer walls. The house will be decorated with wood carvings and sculptures.

This winter home is one of a village of thirty houses. In summer, it will be empty, its occupants gone to the salmon-fishing grounds. With the cold weather, they will return.

Based on the available anthropological evidence, that is an accurate description of house construction on the British Columbia coast before the arrival of Europeans, and it shows that Indian civilization was flourishing in Canada at the time. Yet today the image that many Canadians have of native people is that they are lazy, shiftless, often drunk, always getting into trouble, and riding high on the government gravy train. There is no denying that Canada's native people face economic and social problems, many of them rooted in the treatment they received when Canada was being colonized. One fact stands out — as an identifiable group Canada's native people are at the bottom of the economic scale. They have been, are now and are likely to remain the poorest of Canada's poor for a long time to come.

Poverty brings with it a host of social problems ranging from a greater likelihood of trouble with the law to the lack of a sense of self-worth. The income of the average Indian family is only one-half to two-thirds that of the average Canadian family. The life expectancy of the average Indian is approximately ten years less than that of the average Canadian. An Indian is three times as likely to be incarcerated as his white counterpart. The school completion rate for the Indian population is less than one-quarter of the national average. Unemployment on some reserves is as high as 90 per cent. Accidents, violence and poisonings are the primary causes of death among Indian people, three times higher than the national rate. Rates of suicide are six times the national average. And there are many other problems besides these.

To compound these problems the 1960s and 1970s saw a large-scale migration of Indian people to urban centres, a migration that is still continuing and that in the sixties was encouraged by the federal government, although what Indians found in the cities was unemployment, discrimination and a social structure that was unable to cope with their needs. Such traditional pursuits as hunting were of course abandoned by urbanized Indians and it became more difficult to maintain the extended family. The result has been that many Indian people have ended up in poverty ghettos, which have even less to offer than the reserve. Today, over 30 per cent of Canada's Indians live in an urban setting. Estimates are that by the 1990s the figure will climb to 50 per cent. Moreover, whether in urban or rural areas, the story of poverty and deprivation is equally true for Canada's Métis and Inuit people.

It is not only in Canada that Indian and other native peoples find themselves at the bottom of the economic heap. The situation is the same in the United States, Norway, Peru, Ecuador, Chile, Bolivia, Nicaragua, New Zealand, Australia and any other nation with a population of aboriginal people. Australian Aborigines form 1 per cent of the population but 30 per cent of the prison population. Their school completion rate is less than one-third the national rate. In some Central and South American nations the economic gap between non-natives and natives is far wider than in Canada. In Peru (where 40 per cent of the population is Indian) the gardened and walled mansions of Lima's pricy European suburbs are a far cry from the cardboard Indian shanties by the airport. In other Central and Southern American countries it is not only poverty that Indians face. Forced relocation, concentration camps and even genocide are commonplace.

Grinding poverty, alcoholism and social conflict were not always part of Indian life. Prior to European discovery, the peoples of the Americas were proud and self-reliant. There were highly sophisticated civilizations — even by European standards — in Mexico (the Aztecs, the Mayas, and others) and in Peru (the Inca). Organized urban life was also found in parts of the United States such as Arizona, New Mexico and the Mississippi Valley. Villages were in existence in parts of southern Canada, on the B.C. coast, and in the Arctic. Crop cultivation was common in many parts of the Americas, including southern Ontario. Even the nomadic tribes of the Canadian prairies had developed societal organizations.

Why have the descendants of these proud civilizations been reduced to dependence on the state, to poverty, to alcoholism and to other evils of European civilization? The Indians of Peru have a phrase to explain how this happened. They call it "world reversal". To understand this "world reversal" it is necessary to go back to the first settlement of the Americas.

The Peopling of the Americas

There is general agreement amongst anthropologists that human beings are not indigenous to the Americas. There is far less agreement about when, how and why man came to the Americas. The view of most anthropologists is that somewhere between 40,000 and 100,000 years ago, people from Siberia and Manchuria began to move across a land bridge in the area of what is now the Bering Strait. However, even without a land bridge, movement across the strait would have been possible, as it is covered with ice seven to eight months of the year and is dotted with islands.

No one knows why these people migrated, how many they were and over what period of time the movement took place. There has been some suggestion, for example, that there may have been movement of Inuit people from Siberia as recently as 1,000 years ago, yet the move must have begun thousands of years before that. It is difficult to conceive of the spread of people across the two Americas, and the development of sophisticated cultures like the Inca, all stemming from a small one-time migration.

It is believed that much of North America was covered with ice at the time of the arrival of the first human beings. This may have forced movement southward. Even during the glacial period there were probably a few north-south strips of land not covered with ice, which would have lent themselves to southward movement. As the ice receded, perhaps some of the latecomers decided to remain in Canada.

Around 11,000 years ago these migrants were hunting on the Canadian plains. Recently, archeologists discovered a campsite on Winnipeg River, which they believe to be over 8,000 years old; it was probably used annually during a two-week period each fall.

The migration theory leaves many questions unanswered; it meant a very rapid movement of people across the two Americas, and a remarkable adaptation to widely different conditions of climate and environment, ranging from Arctic to tropical. By 1000 B.C., fairly sophisticated cultures existed in what is today Peru. Crop cultivation in Mexico began somewhere between 2500 and 3000 B.C. If migration began about 100,000 years ago, how did humanity spread so quickly from the Arctic to mountaintop cities in Peru? The dispersal of man in Europe, Asia and Africa took place over a much greater period of time, perhaps even millions of years.

To put such a migration into perspective it must be remembered that there is still no road leading from Nome, Alaska, to the southern tip of South America. Both the wheel and the horse were introduced to the

Americas by the Europeans. Without them, the migrant peoples must have travelled on foot and by water.

Another unanswered question is the development of languages. Today there are eleven main Indian language groups in Canada, and no common root has been found for them. How did people migrating from the same part of the world develop such distinct languages? Along with distinct languages, distinct cultures developed. There is a tendency amongst non-natives to think of Indians as one cultural group. The name *Indian* has no justification other than Christopher Columbus's belief that he had discovered India. In pre-European times one was not an Indian; rather one was a Cree, a Malecite, a Haida and so forth.

One explanation of the cultural and linguistic diversity that developed in the Americas is that some peoples there had contact with other parts of the world. Some anthropologists believe that there were sea contacts across the South Pacific between the Melanesian Islands and the Americas. Such contacts, if they occurred, probably did not involve a massive movement of people, but may have involved the exchange of technology, culture and social influences. One anthropologist suggests there are parallels in grammatical structure and vocabulary between some of the Melanesian dialects and the Hokan group in California. Early Pacific explorers commented on the similarities between the forts, carved house-poles (totem poles), whalebone clubs and cedar-bark beaters of British Columbia and the forts, house-ports and clubs of New Zealand and the tapa-cloth of central Polynesia. And one anthropologist has found considerable similarities between some of the ceremonies in Melanesia and the potlatch (a ceremony in which one gives away one's goods and acquisitions) in British Columbia.

Development of Indian Settlements in the Americas

Little is known about the development of Indian settlements in this hemisphere. There are several reasons for this. Other than amongst the Mayas, writing had not been developed in the Americas when the Europeans arrived. Indians relied on oral history, aided by various memory devices such as strings of wampum and strings with knots. Europeans were taught to rely on written records and thus dismissed the Indians as having no past.

Also prevalent, on the part of the Europeans, whether English, Spanish or French, was an ethnocentric attitude that European civilization was the only truly human mode of existence and that any other culture was barbarous and aberrant. Missionaries, explorers and soldiers saw it as their duty to tame the savages and introduce civilization among them. There was even a debate amongst Spanish theologians in the sixteenth century as to whether Indians were rational and possessed souls. Much of what was Indian was wantonly destroyed; the Spanish razed many Inca and Aztec cities and destroyed all other signs of civilization they found, fearing that the Inca and Aztec cities were the Devil's work.

Lest one dismiss such actions as solely the action of brutal Spanish conquistadors, it should be remembered that in the 1950s the Canadian government forcibly moved whole Inuit communities hundreds of miles to place them in government-established centres. On the Canadian prairies Indian children were removed from their families, placed in residential schools and punished if they spoke their native language.

Thus, over the course of several hundred years a conscious effort was made to eradicate any knowledge of the history of man in the Americas prior to the arrival of the Europeans. Even today, many Canadian history texts start with the arrival of Columbus in America, leaving the impression that human civilization in the Americas only began with the coming of the whites. However, in spite of the sparsity of the written historical record, certain things are known.

In the 1500s (during the Spanish conquest of the Americas) many cities in Central and South America were larger than those found in Spain at the same time. Tenochtitlan, the Aztec capital, over which Mexico City was built, is estimated to have had a population of 200,000 when it was conquered by the Spanish. Neighbouring Teotihuacan, dating from a pre-Aztec civilization, is estimated to have had a population of 125,000 at its zenith. Running water was common in many Inca, Aztec and Mayan cities at a time when open sewers were the order of the day in most European cities. The Inca road network extended over what is today part of five South American nations. Inca stoneworkers fitted together stones of different sizes, without mortar, to make solid walls, with an ingenuity no one has yet been able to duplicate. The Incas had a system of social security that ensured that the handicapped, the aged and children were cared for. Crime was virtually non-existent and every able-bodied person was required to contribute to society.

The height to which some Indian civilizations in the Americas had soared can be judged from the words of the Spanish soldier Bernal Díaz. In his *The True History of the Conquest of New Spain* Díaz states:

> ...when we saw so many cities and villages...we couldn't restrain our admiration. It was like the enchantments told about in the book of Amadis,

because of the high towers, churches, and other buildings, all of masonry, which rose from the water....Then
when we entered Iztapalapa, the appearance of the
palaces in which they quartered us! They were vast,
and well made of cut stone, cedar and other fragrant
woods, with spacious rooms and patios that were
wonderful to see, shaded with cotton awnings...all
was well plastered and bright, with many kinds of
stone with pictures on them...I stood looking, thinking
that never in the world would lands like these be
discovered again, for at that time we had no knowledge of Peru....Today all that was there then is in the
ground, lost, with nothing left at all.

Of course, in 1520 when the Spanish conquered the
area described in the passage above (which is today
Mexico City), there were no large urban centres in
Canada along the lines of those found in Central and
South America. However, it is also clear that many
of the ideas being developed in Mexico were spreading
northward. Evidence of urban settlements has been
found in various places in North America. For example, several historians suggest that in 1000 A.D. the
city of Cahokia, in the Mississippi Valley near present-
day St. Louis, contained more inhabitants than London,
England. By the time of European colonization Indian
villages had developed in the St. Lawrence valley/
southern Ontario area, in the Arctic and on the British
Columbia coast. Advanced construction techniques had
been developed in the west coast villages. Captain
Cook reported that when he landed at Cape Newen-
ham, British Columbia, in 1778 he was taken into a
house which was 150 feet in length, 24 to 30 feet wide
and 7 to 8 feet high.

What distinguished the Indians of Latin and South
America from their northern counterparts was their

degree of social organization. The Indians in Mexico and Peru had organized themselves into nation-states, while for the most part the political organizations of their northern counterparts remained at the tribal level. The development of nation-states meant that the Incas, Aztecs and Mayas did not have to devote all their energies to food production and gathering. The state could organize food gathering into a more efficient operation, freeing manpower for the building of public works (such as temples and highways) and for the maintenance of an army. Of course, the harsh Canadian climate made it more difficult to find food, leaving less time for political organization.

Indian Life in Canada Prior to European Discovery

It is estimated that approximately 6 to 10 million people lived in North America between 1000 and 1500 A.D., 250,000 of them in what is today Canada. The most populous areas were the Windsor-Montreal corridor and the coast of British Columbia. Between 10,000 and 50,000 people are estimated to have lived on the prairies and in the north. With the exception of the people in southern Ontario and Quebec, and on the coast of British Columbia, Indian peoples were nomadic, moving to keep up with the sources of food (usually game). However, distances travelled were usually limited and there is evidence that even the nomadic tribes returned regularly to the same campgrounds. It is estimated that horses were introduced into Canada between 1690 and 1750 on the Canadian plains; they enabled Indians to travel more extensively and made the search for food easier.

With the exception of several hundred square kilometres in the foothills of the Rocky Mountains, between the sources of the Saskatchewan and Athabasca Rivers, all of Canada was occupied or claimed by one or more tribes. Of course, this didn't mean that every area of the country was inhabited; rather that every area of the country was used or claimed by a tribe as its hunting or camping ground. In the case of nomadic tribes a particular area might be visited only once every few years. The important point is that Canada remained undiscovered by the Europeans for a very long time; by the time the Europeans arrived Canada had already been explored, claimed and utilized by the first inhabitants. There was no virgin, uninhabited land for European explorers to claim. Lands wanted by the Europeans had to be bought, leased or taken by force from the original inhabitants. Sometimes the land was taken by exterminating the original people. In addition to the Beothuks of Newfoundland, at least three other Canadian tribes are extinct (the Tobacco, Neutral and Tsetsaut).

Diamond Jenness, a Canadian ethnologist, estimated that there were probably over fifty different tribes in Canada (incidentally, the name Canada comes from the Huron-Iroquois word meaning a village or place where people live) each with their own language and customs. These languages could in turn be grouped into eleven major linguistic stocks. Two of these stocks, Algonkian and Athapaskan, covered nine-tenths of Canada. British Columbia was a babel of tongues with the languages spoken falling into six different linguistic stocks. Linguistic differences did not always mean cultural differences. Communication between the tribes occurred in many ways: sometimes by sign language, sometimes through the use of prisoners as interpreters; and sometimes, too, through neighbourly contact, members of a tribe would learn the language of their neighbours.

Various food foraging techniques were developed. Fish weirs, made from branches and animal skins, were common in many parts of the country. Canoes were paddled into wild rice patches and the rice shaken into the canoe. Buffalo traps were developed on the prairies. A yelling band would surround a herd of buffalo and drive the animals over a cliff or other natural drop. Sometimes, if there was no natural drop, a semi-circular corral was constructed on the open plain. Women, children and fast runners were responsible for driving the herd into the corral. The best marksmen would be hidden behind the corral and would spring up for the kill as the herd entered the corral.

Indians used natural resources efficiently. They killed only what they needed and made use of every part of the carcass. Obtaining food, in the days before the introduction of the gun, was a major effort. Indians did not have the technology or the human resources to indulge in sport killing and could not afford the luxury of inefficiency. They respected nature and natural resources, not only because it was the source of their livelihood but also because Indians believed that all things possessed life and that all life was one. All things possessed spirits and it was wrong to kill spirits needlessly.

Religion played an important part in the lives of all Indians, nomadic or settled. Usually each tribe had a Great Spirit (the name varied from tribe to tribe) along with various other spirits. Spirits were personifications of mysterious forces (the rising sun, the wind, the changing seasons) which Indians saw working around them and which they could not understand. Offerings were made to the spirits. While human sacrifices were common amongst the Aztecs and Incas, they were extremely rare amongst Canadian Indians. Indian religious beliefs centred around explaining the unknown and various natural phenomena. Indians believed that the sun, moon, wind, water, animals and even people were influenced by the spirits. Because of the importance of his environment the Indian sought to live in harmony with his surroundings.

Some Indians seemed to have a closer link with the spirits, as evidenced by trances. These often became medicine men or shamans. In some areas medicine lodges (guilds of medicine men) were common. In British Columbia religious societies, often restricted to nobles, were common.

The popular image of Indian tribes is that they were constantly engaged in war. Such was not the case. Survival and food gathering were the most important activities. War was not engaged in for idle reasons. When it did occur it often arose out of a conflict over hunting grounds. The image (due largely to Hollywood) of Indian wars with thousands of massacres is simply not true.

The Cree leader Saukamappee described to the explorer David Thompson a war he had taken part in against the Shoshones in the 1720s. Thompson recounts the story in his memoirs (*David Thompson's Narrative*, edited by Richard Glover).

> After some singing and dancing, they [the Shoshones] sat down on the ground, and placed their large shields before them, which covered them: We did the same,...On both sides several were wounded, but none lay on the ground; and night put an end to the battle without a scalp being taken by either side, and in those days such was the result, unless one party was more numerous than the other.

This was a time when the standard tactic in European warfare was for the opposing armies to march towards each other with guns blazing. Of course, Indian warfare changed with the introduction of the horse and gun. The point is that Indians were not warlike savages. They were probably less and certainly no more warlike than the Europeans.

Indian Governments in Canada Before European Settlement

Governmental organization beyond the tribal level was evolving in Canada by the time of European discovery of North America. By the end of the sixteenth century the Iroquoian tribes of southern Ontario and western Quebec were grouped into three confederacies, which were eventually (through war) replaced by the League of the Iroquois. Tribes composing the League remained independent in domestic matters, but delegated authority in external matters (inter-tribal feuds, war, trade) to a council of some fifty chiefs, who met as the need arose. The Haudenosaunee (meaning People of the Longhouse — as the Iroquois called themselves) had developed a formalized constitution, which was recited every five years by elders who had committed it to memory. It provided for a democratic system that allowed each extended family to select two senior leaders, one female and one male, to speak at councils. The constitution had rules of debate which ensured that a consensus would be reached. Laws were passed at bicameral (two-chambered) legislative sittings. It is impossible to guess where this political structure would have led had it not been for the arrival of the Europeans. Perhaps temples, government buildings constructed out of masonry and a sophisticated society would have developed in another century or two. As Diamond Jenness, who spent his life studying Canada's aboriginal people, put it, "they [the Iroquoian nations] had the spirit of empire builders, although their empire, like the glow of sunrise in an Arctic winter, faded away before it reached full brightness." It faded with the coming of the Europeans.

Political and social structures had also evolved on the west coast. Semi-permanent villages had developed, and the village was the basic political unit. Within each, three classes existed: the nobles, the commoners and the slaves (generally prisoners of war). The villages were divided into houses, with everyone of common ancestry belonging to the same house. Each house was headed by a noble and also had its commoners and slaves. The nobles and their houses were also graded, and the rank of each was indicated by the seat he occupied at feasts and potlatches. A noble's position on the social scale carried with it certain privileges, such as the ownership of a fishing weir or hunting territory, the right to sing a certain song or execute a certain dance, or perhaps the right to paint and erect a certain form of totem pole. In contrast to the Iroquoian nations, the west coast Indians' political organization had not evolved beyond the village level. Organizational efforts on the west coast were largely devoted to festivals, ceremonies and other social activities.

While Indian social and political organizations in other parts of Canada had not evolved to the same extent, native peoples there were not living in chaos. In most of Canada (the north, the prairies, northern Ontario and Quebec), food was not as plentiful as it was in southern Ontario, the St. Lawrence valley area, or the west coast. The Indians inhabiting the plains and the north had not developed cultivation, and consequently much of their energies were focused on food gathering. They did not have the leisure time or people power to develop more elaborate social and political structures.

Amongst most of the nomadic Indians the basic social and political organization was the band, which could be likened to an extended family. Linguistic, cultural and marital ties, and the sharing of hunting grounds, often brought bands together into loose tribal affiliations. However, the tribe became much more important after the coming of the Europeans. The tribes were not united under common rule like the tribes of Africa or Polynesia; the authority of the tribal chief was at best uncertain and in many cases non-existent. Social and political organizations were more highly developed amongst the Indians of the plains than they were amongst the nomadic tribes of maritime Canada.

In the nomadic tribes, decisions were generally made by consensus of the fully grown males of the tribe. Such tribes usually lived a life of plenty and comfort. Male members of the band occupied themselves with the hunt while female members busied themselves with domestic functions. Much, however, depended on the hunt and occasional famines occurred.

All Indian bands and tribes had chiefs and many Plains Indians had semi-military secret societies (secret societies exist even today in some bands), which performed various functions. For example, one such group might serve as a policing body to maintain law and order.

Tribes often moved, and not only within their own hunting areas. Occasionally they were forced, for reasons still unknown, to migrate to different parts of the continent. The Navajo moved southwestward to occupy their territory in New Mexico and Arizona.

The Assiniboines (now in southeastern Saskatchewan and southern Manitoba) moved from the south in the 1600s. The Sarcees (now near Calgary) moved from the north. Some of the Iroquoian tribes moved from the Ohio valley to southern Ontario. Some of the Cree moved from the Hudson's Bay area into the Canadian plains. The Ojibwa also moved from the Hudson's Bay area to western Ontario and eastern Manitoba.

The Coming of the Europeans

Probably the factor with the greatest influence over the movement of Indian people was the coming of the Europeans. The establishment of settlements and the demands of the fur trade forced Indians to move, sometimes to get away from settlements, and sometimes to get more or better furs to trade. In the United States some Indians were forced-marched out of the southeastern states.

The coming of the Europeans meant much more than relocation. It meant a total transformation of life for the Indians. European ethnocentricity was unable to accept that things could be done other than the European way. If Indians were to be allowed to exist, then the assumption was that Indian authority structures and values had to be replaced with European values, through the efforts of missionaries, educators, government agents, soldiers and police. However, it was not a given that Indians should be allowed to survive. In 1841 Herman Merivale, who later became permanent undersecretary at the Colonial Office in London, outlined four alternatives for dealing with native people: extermination, slavery, insulation and amalgamation. After discussing these four alternatives he outlined his hopes that the Indian could be absorbed into Canadian society through intermarriage.

Almost every aspect of Indian life was touched and dramatically changed with the coming of the Europeans. Indians were not allowed time to integrate at their own pace with European settlement. Like the great cities of Central and South America, everything the Indians had was destroyed, and replaced with a way of life that meant nothing to them.

The Europeans came to exploit the resources of the Americas and they made use of Indians to help them. This was a dramatic change from the Indian's traditional relationship to the land. For example, European traders kept demanding more furs. This meant that both Indians and white trappers tended to overtrap. As the furbearing animals were reduced in an area, trappers were forced to move to another unexploited area to maintain the same level of fur production. The difference in attitude between whites and Indians was described by Ralph Parsons, fur trade commissioner of the Hudson's Bay Company, in a 1937 Canadian Press article (reprinted in *As Long as This Land Shall Last*, by René Fumoleau).

> Very few white people, taking up trapping as an occupation, give any thought to conservation. The great majority take up trapping in the same way as they would take up any other occupation — to obtain the largest possible return in the shortest possible time....The Indian...will only take what he requires to see him through from day to day....With few exceptions, it will be found that where Indians have been left alone, there is no undue scarcity of animal life in the vicinity.

Ironically, white hunters, trappers and conservationists today complain that Indians are overhunting and destroying all the game animals.

Indian values and traditions suffered the same fate as the Indian relationship to resources. After some discussion colonial policy-makers decided the way to deal with Indians was to civilize them. In other words, Indian religion and values had to be destroyed and replaced with European ones. The tactics used were often brutal.

The Spanish even resorted to military force to Christianize Indians. In 1690 Father Francisco Viva, with the consent of the Bishop of Quito (in Ecuador) commenced a military attack against the Jivaros Indians. His goal was to Christianize the Indians for the Spanish Crown. Several years later a bitter and disappointed Father Viva reported, ''In five years we have succeeded in bringing 1,630 Jivaros out of their hiding places, but what spiritual benefit has been gained? Many of these captives despair and hang themselves, others in desperation die by refusing food and drink, others stuff sticks in their throats and choke themselves... When all is said and done, the Jivaros are like brute animals.''

Almost two centuries later, Lieutenant-Governor Alexander Morris, who was responsible for negotiating four Indian treaties in western Canada, reported, ''But the churches too have their duties to fulfil. There is common ground between the Christian churches and the Indians, as they all believe as we do, in a Great Spirit. The transition thence to the Christian's God is an easy one...And now I close. Let us have Christianity and civilization to leaven the mass of heathenism and paganism among Indian tribes....''

It was not only Indian religious beliefs that suffered. Various Indian cultural practices and traditions were outlawed by federal legislation in Canada. For over seventy years, commencing in the 1880s, the potlatch ceremony practised by Haida and other tribes of north-western B.C. was outlawed. This ceremony involves giving away property; thus it was seen as discouraging Indians from adopting European attitudes to property, that is, individual ownership. Various dances like the sundance were outlawed. In 1914 the Indian Act made it illegal for any western Canadian Indian to appear outside his or her reserve in "aboriginal costume" unless the Indian agent had given his permission.

Perhaps the ultimate sanction was that a federal law, the Indian Act, defined who was an Indian. This was such a botched effort that it made some white women into Indians by marriage and turned many Indians into non-Indians. The latter are often referred to as non-status Indians as they have no status under the Indian Act. The federal government finally got around to rectifying some of these injustices with the 1985 changes to the Indian Act.

The introduction of European technology also had a profound effect on Indian life. The rifle not only made it easier for the Indian to obtain food but also dramatically changed the nature of feuds and wars. Previously unheard-of death tolls now resulted from minor skirmishes.

Having to cope with new technology, new ideas, the destruction of one's culture and the introduction of a new religion, all without one's consent, requires strength. However, when Indians most needed such strength they were devastated by the introduction of alcohol and European diseases. Smallpox, typhus, tuberculosis and sexually transmitted diseases quickly depleted the Indian population. Typhus destroyed one-third of the Micmacs in Acadia in the 1700s and all of the Inuit on Southampton Island in Hudson's Bay in the early 1900s. In the 1780s smallpox is estimated to have wiped out nine-tenths of the Chipewyan population of the Northwest Territories. Another smallpox epidemic raged through the Canadian plains in 1837-38. The epidemic, coupled with the reduction of the buffalo and the ensuing starvation, greatly reduced the number of Indians on the Canadian plains.

Equally devastating was the effect of alcohol. The Indians themselves were very concerned about alcohol. As reported by Alexander Morris, who negotiated four of the treaties in western Canada,

> The treaties all provide for the exclusion of the sale of spirits, or ''fire-water'', on the reserves. The Indians themselves know their weakness. Their wise men say, ''If it is there we will use it, give us a strong law against it.''

It was in part to control the liquor trade and the violence resulting from it that in 1873 the federal government formed the North-West Mounted Police (forerunners of the RCMP) and sent them to the Canadian prairies.

Considering all these factors it is not difficult to see why the Indians in Peru came up with the phrase ''world reversal'' to describe what happened to them upon the coming of the Spanish. Indian people in Canada are only now beginning to recover from the reversal of their world.

Changing Attitudes to Indians

After the arrival of Europeans native life can be divided into four eras. First there was a short era when Europeans considered Indians their equals. This was followed by another short period when Europeans began to reject the idea that Indians were equal to them. After that, for centuries, Europeans regarded the Indian as an inferior being, and believed that it was their duty to civilize the savage. The fourth era is the cultural and political resurgence of Indian people, which is occurring now.

The first era of equality was not based on brotherly love but on necessity. When Europeans first arrived in North America, they were few in number and not always fitted for life on the new continent. Matters were also complicated by the fact that various European nations were competing for territory in North America. Under such circumstances it was helpful to have friends on the continent.

The Indians were actively used by European nations to raid the settlements of competing powers, and as allies in war. For example, in the early 1720s the French encouraged a number of tribes in the maritime region to harass the English colonies. New France was never heavily populated (its total population was 75,000 when it surrendered to the British in 1760), and was thus very dependent on its Indian allies. Many of the alliances were very informal; often Indians were given goods in return for harassing the enemy.

After the fall of New France the British tended to draw upon the Indians to help them in their fights with the Americans; Indians south of what became the international border aided the British in the War of 1812. As a result of the war the Americans moved many Indians away from the border to ensure that they would not be influenced by the British.

However, it was not only as allies in war that the Indians served the Europeans. It was from Indians that early settlers learned how to survive in the harsh Canadian climate. They learned about transportation: the canoe, the snowshoe, the navigable river routes. They also adopted many Indian foods, such as pumpkins, squash, beans and maize. Wild rice, today a delicacy on Canadian tables, was a staple for some Indians. Tobacco, a drug used by millions, was also cultivated by the Indians and adopted by the Europeans.

An early Ukrainian settler on the Canadian prairies told the story of working in the field clearing land by hand when an elderly Indian came by.

> He got off his horse and walked over to a clump of bush. He was talking in some kind of language but I couldn't understand anything. He waved to me to come over. I was kind of scared and didn't go at first. Finally I went and as I got nearer I saw that he was eating these berries. Slowly, he picked off a berry and dropped it into his mouth. He was showing me I should do the same. I finally did and tasted the juiciest berry I had ever had. I smiled and tried to thank the man. Food was not exactly plentiful and I was more than happy to learn about some edible berries. I will always remember that incident and wonder why today [1957] we always think of the Indian in such a bad way.

The berry was the Saskatoon berry, a prairie delicacy.

Indians also helped lead the European colonists across the continent. Every school child has had to memorize the names of Canada's famous explorers; Champlain, La Salle, La Verendrye, Thompson, Kelsey, MacKenzie, Fraser and so on. However, all of these explorers had Indians with them who acted not only as guides but also as intermediaries with other tribes. And it was from the Indians that explorers learned the locations of rivers, seas and lakes.

In the early days of the fur trade, too, the Indians not only trapped and delivered furs but also acted as guides, advancemen and agents. For example, the Cree on the Canadian plains often traded with the Blackfoot, whose lands were further west, then delivered the pelts to the Hudson's Bay Company. Métis gradually replaced the Indians as traders.

But the era of friendship and alliance was not a long one. The role of the Indians in Canada rapidly declined with changes in the fur trade. The Métis were playing a greater role and the fur trade itself was in decline. Europeans had developed strategies for survival in Canada and were no longer dependent upon Indians to teach them survival techniques. Wars were no longer being fought, and so Indian allies were no longer needed. Thus ended the short era of semi-equality.

Following this was a short era when equality was destroyed, then a long era of inequality. Both were marked by a conscious attempt to destroy the Indian identity and replace it with the identity of the "good civilized Canadian". Cultural practices were legislated against; attempts were made to Christianize Indians; reserves were established so Indians could learn agriculture and other ways in which they could be useful to Canadian society. Indians could not become lawyers, doctors or ministers and keep their Indian status. Children were taken to residential schools many kilometres away in order to remove them from the Indian atmosphere and to ensure that they were inculcated with the right values. Nor did the half-bloods, the Métis, fare any better. While a great number of Métis were employed by the Hudson's Bay Company, very few were hired other than as labourers. Almost no Métis made it to the officer rank of the company.

Throughout these two eras, which in the west and in northern Ontario lasted from the 1860s to the 1960s and in eastern Canada from the early 1800s to the 1960s, there was considerable conflict over what role

Indians could be expected to play in Canadian society. Some believed that once the Indian was broken of his old ways he could be assimilated into the mainstream of Canadian society. There were others, however, who believed that, no matter how much civilizing was done, the Indian would never be able to become a part of Canadian society because he was not the equal of the white man.

Cultural and political resurgence began in the 1960s. The sixties were a decade of political action when North Americans began re-examining their complacent attitudes to social questions. Royal commissions were examining offical bilingualism and the status of women. Black rights became a crucial issue in the United States. In Canada, war was declared on poverty; Pierre Trudeau came to power promising a just society; liberal thinkers began to advocate changes in society, to deal better with the needs of the poor and minorities. A government study revealed that the federal government had not been successful in its policies dealing with Indians. The Indian-Eskimo Association was formed in Toronto in the early 1960s to bring native issues to public attention. The political climate of the sixties was a favourable one for the championing of native rights. The issue itself was, of course, far from being an invention of the sixties but it was during that decade that the native situation gained public prominence.

In the late sixties the federal government introduced a new policy, which was announced in a White Paper. Ottawa's answer to improving the social situation of Canada's Indians was to abolish Indian treaties, reserves and status. The paper achieved the opposite effect: threatened with the extinction of their culture and status, Indians began to organize politically and become more vocal in seeking protection of their rights.

The political resurgence of the 1960s is now beginning to bear fruit. Native issues have caught the attention of Canada's media. Serious land claims negotiations are under way in many areas of Canada. Many
Canadians have accepted that native people should
have some degree of self-government. And perhaps
the greatest achievement was the mention of native
rights in Canada's new Constitution. The draft agreement on the Constitution, reached on November 5,
1981, did not mention native rights. However, after
lobbying, trips to Britain by native leaders, court action
and public statements, the draft, which became Canada's Constitution on April 17, 1982, was revised to
provide that ''The existing aboriginal and treaty rights
of the aboriginal peoples of Canada are hereby recognized and affirmed.'' The Constitution defines aboriginal people as including ''...the Indian, Inuit and Métis
peoples of Canada''.

Who Are Canada's First People?

There are approximately 1,100,000 native people in
Canada: 330,000 status Indians (it is estimated that
the 1985 changes in defining Indian status will add
some 60,000 to 75,000 people to that figure, putting
them back on the Indian roll), 750,000 Métis and non-
status Indians (less whatever number become status
Indians under the 1985 changes to the Indian Act) and
25,000 Inuit. All of these figures are estimates. While
all status Indians are registered under various band
lists or in the general Indian register, the figures
provided by the Department of Indian Affairs do not
always agree with the figures given by Statistics
Canada. Some mixed-blood people are registered as
status Indians and, until 1985, white women who

married Indian men could also be registered as Indians. The non-status Indians are those who gave up their status or lost it (until 1985 status could be voluntarily given up) or for whatever reason were never registered by the Indian Affairs bureaucracy — perhaps the family was out on the hunt when the registration took place. At Lubicon Lake, in northern Alberta, federal and provincial officals disagreed during a 1985 dispute over how many more people were entitled to be registered as Indians. Their figures differed by over 300 individuals; ex-federal Justice Minister Davey Fulton was called in to mediate the dispute.

Most of Canada's status Indian people are registered with one of the approximately 550 bands in Canada. While reserves have been set aside for most bands it is estimated that over 30 per cent of Canada's status Indians live in urban centres. Most reserves in Canada, unlike those in the United States, are very small. There are 2,240 reserves in Canada (some bands have more than one reserve) totalling 2,428,200 hectares (6 million acres). The largest Indian reserve in Canada is the Blood Reserve in southern Alberta covering approximately 1,386 square kilometres (535 square miles) and having a population of 4,600. By comparison, nearby Banff National Park covers an area of 6640 square kilometres (2,564 square miles).

The status Indian population is spread fairly evenly throughout the central and western provinces. On a province-by-province basis the Indian population is: British Columbia, 55,000; Alberta, 36,000; Saskatchewan, 45,000; Manitoba, 44,000; Ontario, 67,000; Quebec, 31,000; New Brunswick, 3,500; Nova Scotia, 4,000; Prince Edward Island, 500; Newfoundland, unknown; Yukon, 4,000; Northwest Territories, 8,000. The current Indian birth rate is approximately twice the national birth rate; the Indian population is increasing.

The term *métis* is used in two ways; to refer to all mixed-blood people and also to refer to the descendants of the Métis nation of the Red River Valley. The latter almost all live in western Canada (mostly in Manitoba, Alberta, Saskatchewan and the Northwest Territories). The number of Métis and non-status Indians in Canada is a source of debate; there has never been an accurate count and estimates vary between 200,000 and 800,000.

Because of the scarcity of data it is difficult to determine the non-status/Métis population in each province.

Most of Canada's Inuit live in the Arctic, north of the tree line. They refer to their land as Nunavut (meaning "our land") and are the majority of the population in that area, making an Inuit province a distinct possibility in the future.

The 1,100,000 Indian, Inuit and Métis people are the descendants of Canada's first people. These are the people who occupied, colonized and in some cases settled almost all of Canada before its discovery by the Europeans. Often they were dispossessed of their lands; sometimes they sold their land for less than adequate compensation. It is not surprising that the land issue is the most important native rights question in Canada today.

2
The Recognition of Native Rights

The plaque at Fort Frontenac in Kingston, Ontario, reads:

The Crawford Purchase

In October 1783, at Carleton Island near here, Captain Redford Crawford of King's Royal Regiment of New York met with local Missassauga Indians, led by elderly Mynass. Crawford acting for the British government, purchased from the Missassauga for some clothing, ammunition and coloured cloth a large tract of land East of Bay of Quinte...

It is a succinct statement about Indian land rights in North America. It bears witness to the long-standing British policy, adopted almost the day the British cast anchor in the Americas, of buying land from the Indians. From the Indian perspective the plaque is a reminder that they rarely got a square deal. They gave away a lot of Canada for a few trinkets and a couple of plugs of tobacco.

Land issues are the key to native politics today. It was land that brought hundreds of Cree and Inuit from James Bay, many of whom spoke no French or English and had never been in a city before, to a Montreal courtroom in 1972. They had come to take part in the court proceedings that halted the James Bay project and eventually forced the Quebec and federal governments to pay heed to native rights. It was also a land rights issue that brought the Inuit of Baker Lake to a federal courtroom to complain about mining companies scaring off their caribou. Indians, Inuit and Métis came for the same reason to speak to Tom Berger's Mackenzie Valley Pipeline Inquiry in the mid-seventies. And since then the list of interventions, both in court and out of court, by native people struggling to protect their traditional hunting and fishing grounds has grown. That list includes disputes at Meares Island, off the west coast, where Macmillan Bloedel was seeking logging rights and where members of the Opitsat and Ahousat bands had camped to prevent such logging; Lyell Island, in the Queen Charlotte Islands, where Haida Indians physically blocked logging trucks; the Norman Wells pipeline; Lubicon Lake; the double-tracking of the CNR line through British Columbia; Kitwanga in northwestern British Columbia, where the Gitwangak Indian band blockaded CN's maintenance yards; and many others. As more of Canada's frontier areas are opened to development, the list will grow.

There are several important questions at the heart of this issue. What land do native people own? If they own land what rights do they have over the land? Do they, for example, own the mineral and water rights on that land? Finally, what rights do they have to control activity on their land? Do they have the right to govern their own territories?

As far as native people are concerned they were the owners of the Americas when the Europeans arrived. Native notions of land centred on the community; it was for use by the community and was a source of food and support. Their concept of land was holistic;

the land was not to be exploited but rather was given by the Great Spirit to be used not only by man but also by the animals and plants. One's successors were also believed to have rights in the land, therefore, one had an obligation to leave it for them in the condition in which one had inherited it oneself. Individual ownership of land was unknown, as were such concepts as selling, leasing or mortgaging land. Land was not a commodity of trade in Indian societies (court decisions of the nineteenth and the early twentieth century often stated that Indians had no land rights because they didn't believe in individual ownership — the idea of communal ownership was foreign to European legal systems). Bands and tribes appropriated certain land as their hunting or camping territory; however, there was no strict delineation of territories, and they would be changed as the needs of a band changed.

Euro-Canadian notions of land were and are solidly rooted in the idea of individual ownership. A parcel of land represents a bundle of rights, which can be divided amongst different owners. For example, minerals in land can be owned by one person, and the surface by another. Similarly, a bank holding a mortgage on a parcel of property has rights in that land. With individual ownership, it became necessary to define boundaries and the rights of the owner. This led to the development of a complex legal system to deal with issues such as how to define boundaries, how to prove ownership, how to transfer ownership and how to define rights that other people or institutions (like the bank) might have in the land. With the development of commerce the practice of giving land for security (mortgaging) developed. Over the centuries, the English courts developed rules for dealing with land, rules that were brought to Canada by English settlers and are still a part of Canadian law.

With the discovery of the Americas and their inhabitants, debate began in theological and legal circles as to what rights, if any, these people had. An ancillary question was whether the "New World" had been conquered or discovered. In the 1500s, as today, international law was that if a country was conquered its inhabitants retained their rights (such as the ownership of land) until such time as the conquering power passed a law, issued a proclamation, or by some other act took those rights away. The discovery theory, on the other hand, assumes that the country is uninhabited; therefore, there is no one to claim rights. The Australian courts have taken the view that Australia was "discovered", and have thereby denied that the Aborigines have any rights, in spite of anthropological evidence suggesting that some 300,000 to 600,000 Aborigines lived in Australia at the time of its conquest by England.

Determining whether a land was conquered or discovered necessitated deciding whether it was inhabited by "people". This judgement was made by the standards of the day, which didn't always accept the coloured non-European as the equal of the white European or, for that matter, even as human.

Of course, while this scholarly debate was going on, soldiers and traders in the Americas killed Indians and destroyed their property, or drove them off their land, oblivious to the philosophical debates taking place in Europe. To the soldiers and explorers, Indians were savages and heathens and it was inconceivable that they could be the owners of the land.

Spanish Recognition of Aboriginal Rights

The Spanish conquistadors were particularly brutal — they smashed Indian cities and drove out those Indians they did not kill, then reconquered the survivors and made them into slaves. A feudal system of landholding, called *encomienda*, was developed in the Spanish Americas. Under this system, conquistadors were awarded large land grants (often lands from which the Indians had been expelled) together with the services of Indians who became vassals of the landowners. The conscripted Indians often had to be forcibly moved to the landowner's estate. In addition to providing labour (under conditions that amounted to slavery) Indians were also required to pay tribute to the landowner in products such as cloth, cacao, game animals, cotton, wax and salt. Modified forms of bondage persisted in Mexico's Yucatan Peninsula until well into the 1800s.

Perhaps it was reports of the cruelty of the conquistadors in the Americas, a growing liberalism in Spain, or some other reason, but in the early 1500s a number of Spanish theologians became concerned about the Indian situation in the Americas. The most famous was Francisco de Vitoria, professor of sacred theology at the University of Salamanca. His 1532 public lectures on Indian rights helped change official governmental thinking about Indians. Vitoria argued that Indians were the owners of lands in the Americas. The fact that Indians were not Catholics, he argued, could not affect their land rights. He also discounted the argument that Indians were not intelligent and therefore not capable of owning land. Indians were at least as intelligent as the average Spanish peasant, who could own land, Vitoria argued. Finally, he rejected the discovery theory and said that while the Pope had granted the Americas to Spain and Portugal, the Pope could only grant unoccupied lands. The Americas were occupied by Indians; therefore the Pope's grant was of no effect.

Five years later, in 1537, the Pope, Paul III, issued a Papal Bull that declared:

> ...notwithstanding whatever may have been or may be said to the contrary, the said Indians and all other people who may later be discovered by Christians, are by no means to be deprived of their liberty or the possession of their property, even though they be outside the faith of Jesus Christ;... should the contrary happen, it shall be null and of no effect.

The King of Spain, Charles V, ordered an inquiry into the matter of the rights of the Indians of the Americas. Several years later Spain's Law of the Indies was enacted reflecting the Pope's statement. The law ordered that Indians be placed in a position of equality with Spaniards, and required that Indian lands be protected for Indians. As proved to be the case with subsequent laws protecting Indians, enacted by other European powers, the Spanish Law of the Indies was seldom observed.

The *encomienda* system continued to flourish unabated in parts of Mexico until the 1800s. The legacy of the conquistadors' actions is still very much in evidence in Latin America today. The concept of reserves, land claims negotiation, or protection of Indians is almost unheard of in South and Central America, in spite of the fact that in many of those countries Indians are a significant percentage of the population. Many Indian people of South and Central America find themselves in much the same situation as that faced by their ancestors who had to deal with the

Spanish conquistadors. In Nicaragua, the Sandinista government has forcibly relocated thousands of Miskito, Sumo and Rama Indians. In nearby Guatemala during the 1980s, the World Council of Indigenous Peoples reports, at least 250,000 people, mostly Indian, have been forced to flee government repression; massacres in Indian villages by the Guatemalan security forces have also been reported. In Peru, Indians have found themselves caught in the crossfire of the war between the Shining Path guerillas and the government. The 21,000 Yanomami Indians in Brazil are being wiped out by disease, as the Amazon basin is opened up to development with little regard for the health and welfare of the Indians. Many more examples could be listed.

While the work of early Spanish theologians and government officials had little effect on Indian rights in the Spanish colonies, it influenced other European scholars. The Papal Bull of 1537 and Vitoria's 1532 lectures are often cited today as proof that the European powers, right from the first contact, recognized that the Indians had rights in the land. Hardly a Canadian court case dealing with land rights goes by without the Papal Bull and Vitoria's lectures being quoted.

Of course, not all European powers (even if they were Catholic nations) adopted the official Spanish position in recognizing Indian rights. Another major player in the development of the Americas, France, never recognized Indian land rights. The French position was that the newly discovered lands belonged to the "children of God" and hence, one group of God's children could take the land from another group in order to implant God's word in the land.

The 1612 order appointing Samuel de Champlain lieutenant-governor of New France instructed him to discover gold, minerals, and the Northwest Passage; it also directed him to:

> ...call them, have them instructed, provoke, and move them to the knowledge and service of God and by the light of the Catholic faith and religion, apostolic and Roman, there to establish them in the exercise and profession of it...

The latter duties Champlain left to the various Catholic orders who were given free rein to accomplish these tasks. Lands were granted to the orders, who then established reserves, not out of any recognition that the land belonged to the Indians, but rather with the notion that if Indians could be settled in one location it would be easier to convert them to Catholicism. The Jesuits established the first such reserve in 1637.

England and Aboriginal Rights

The major actor in the development of North America was England. For reasons largely unknown (was it a sense of justice — there was even an Aborigines Protective Society in England — the British sense of order, or political expediency?) British legal scholars and government officials devoted considerable energy to defining their relationship with Indians.

Early English practice in English territories was to grant patents to a trading company to develop, exploit, and sometimes settle an area on behalf of the English Crown. The best-known of such companies was the Hudson's Bay Company. Trading and settlement charters issued to the companies often mentioned Indian rights. Thus, the 1629 letter of instruction sent to Captain John Endicott from the Massachusetts Bay Company stated:

Above all we pray you to be careful that there be none in our precincts permitted to do any injury in the least kind to the heathen people; and if any offend in that way, they themselves receive due correction...if any of the savages pretend right of inheritance to all or any part of the lands granted in our patent we pray you endeavour to purchase their title, that we may avoid the least scruple of intrusion.

In the 1750s France and England fought a war lasting seven years, commonly called the Seven Years' War. Battles were fought on the American continent, culminating in the Battle of the Plains of Abraham, wherein the English General Wolfe defeated the French General Montcalm. The French formally surrendered with the signing of the Articles of Capitulation of Montreal in 1760. Three years later the Treaty of Paris confirmed the surrender of Quebec to England. Following the Treaty, George III, the English king, issued his Royal Proclamation of 1763 dealing with his new lands. The purpose of the Proclamation was to establish four separate governments in the newly acquired territories: the governments of Quebec, Florida, West Florida and Grenada.

The Proclamation also dealt with a number of Indian issues and has become known as the ''Indian Charter of Rights''. It stated that any land within the territorial confines of the new governments that had not been ceded by the Indians ''...are reserved to them, or any of them, as their Hunting Grounds''. The reason that this land was reserved for the Indians was ''...whereas it is just and reasonable, and essential to our Interest, and the Security of our Colonies, that the Several Nations or Tribes of Indians with whom We are connected, and who live under our Protection, should not be molested or disturbed in the Possession...''

The Proclamation also dealt with lands not within the territorial limits of the new governments. It reserved "...for the use of the said Indians, all the Lands and Territories not included within the Limits of Our said Three new Governments, or within the Limits of the Territory granted to the Hudson's Bay Company..." In order to prevent fraud and dissatisfaction amongst Indians the Proclamation also provided a way in which Indian lands could be acquired for settlement. Indian lands "...shall be Purchased only for Us, in our Name, at some public Meeting or Assembly of the said Indians, to be held for that Purpose by the Governor or Commander in Chief of our Colony respectively within which they shall lie..."

By implication the Proclamation suggests that all lands that had not been surrendered by the Indians to the Crown belonged to the Indians. It reserved all unsettled land for the use of the Indians as their hunting grounds. It provided that lands required for settlement had to be bought from the Indians and could only be bought by the Crown at a public meeting. The Royal Proclamation set the stage for the land surrender treaties signed by the Indians and the Crown in Ontario and on the prairies.

Under the Canadian legal system, English laws became a part of the law of Canada on the dates when various colonial governments were formed. Such laws remain in force unless they have been specifically overturned by provincial or federal legislation. Under this rule the Royal Proclamation became a part of Canadian law and is still valid today.

The Proclamation raises a number of questions. Is the Proclamation the source of Indian title or did it merely recognize a pre-existing fact that the land belonged to the Indians? Many Indian leaders and scholars take the latter view; after all, the King had nothing to give to the Indians because the land already belonged to them, so all his Proclamation could do was affirm reality. Territorial limits of the Proclamation have also been a source of debate — did it apply to all of what is today Canada or only to lands that had been discovered by the English up to that date? The colony of British Columbia acted on radically different policies when it came to Indian land rights. Was the colony justified in doing so, or should it have been bound by the Proclamation? Also, significantly, the Proclamation speaks of the "several Nations or Tribes of Indians". Was this an inadvertent use of the word "nation" or was it a recognition that the British were dealing with sovereign Indian nations?

To a large extent the Royal Proclamation was merely restating British policy. Well before the Proclamation, the British had established their policy of requiring that Indian lands be purchased and prohibited their sale to anyone other than an authorized Crown agent. Such policies were not motivated by humanitarian concerns but by political realities. The British were few in number and unfamiliar with the terrain; Indian assistance was necessary to them. Nor were the British interested in fighting a protracted war with the Indians; just prior to the issuance of the Royal Proclamation, Chief Pontiac had led an insurrection at Detroit and the British feared this might be the first of many Indian uprisings.

The Courts Protect Indian Rights

While the Royal Proclamation has often been cited as the bible of aboriginal rights it was but one of many developments, during the settlement of North America, that firmly recognized aboriginal rights. Others included landmark court decisions that recognized Indian land rights. As a result of such court decisions by the Supreme Courts in both Canada and the United States, the concept of Indian land rights is firmly entrenched in the Canadian legal system. While many Canadians may find the notion that much of Canada still belongs to the Indians distasteful, it would require a "world reversal" in Canadian law to take away Indian rights — something that is unlikely to happen in Canada's conservative, precedent-bound legal system.

The first important U.S. Supreme Court decision was the 1823 case involving a dispute between two non-Indians over the ownership of a tract of land that had formerly been Indian land. The defendant, McIntosh, purchased his interest (some 11,500 acres or 4654 hectares) from the United States government in July 1818. The land had been purchased by the British Crown from the Indians prior to the American Revolution. After independence the United States government took possession of all lands belonging to the British Crown. The plaintiff-claimants argued that they held a prior title, which they had acquired from their father and grandfather respectively, who had originally obtained the land as a direct purchase from the Indians.

The Court ruled that the claimants had no right to the land, as they did not have the right to purchase land directly from the Indians. It was a long-standing English policy (as evidenced by the Royal Proclamation of 1763), and one that had been adopted by the United States, that Indian lands had to be purchased and could only be purchased by the government. The Court went on to say that America had been occupied by Indians at the time it was discovered by European powers. Discovery of the continent did not extinguish the rights of the occupants, it merely gave the discovering power the exclusive right to acquire the land from the occupants. The importance of this decision was that it established that Indians had rights in the land and that those rights could only be acquired by government purchase.

Close on the heels of this decision came the United States Supreme Court ruling in Samuel Worcester's case against the State of Georgia. In 1831, Worcester was in Cherokee country, preaching the Gospel to the Indians with permission of the nation's president. About the same time the State of Georgia made it an offence, punishable by four years' hard labour, for anyone to live in Cherokee country without the permission of the state governor: a clear conflict between the president and the governor. The net result, however, was that Worcester was charged with violating Georgian law, and was jailed. He appealed, arguing that Georgia had no jurisdiction over Indian country.

The Supreme Court agreed with Worcester and went on to state that not only did Georgian laws not apply in Indian country but that the only laws that applied were Indian laws. Indian communities were distinct, politically independent entities, retaining their original rights as undisputed possessors of the soil from time immemorial. The only difference that discovery made, according to the Court, was that the Indians' right to govern themselves was limited, but only in that they could deal with no other nation than England and later the United States. In short, the Court described the Indians as dependent nations, free to govern themselves but restricted in their external dealings.

Canada's legal system is based on precedent. Past decisions are looked to for guidance in dealing with new questions. American decisions are not binding on Canadian courts, but they are referred to from time to time for guidance or assistance. In dealing with Indian rights issues, Canadian courts have always started by looking at these two American decisions.

Ironically, while the United States Supreme Court was breaking new ground in defining Indian rights, the American army was driving thousands of Indians, including the Cherokee from Georgia, by forced march to Oklahoma in order to get them out of the way of settlement. Between 1817 and 1850 tens of thousands of Indians and mixed-blood people were expelled from the southeastern states.

The first major Canadian court action involving Indian land arose in the 1880s. In 1873 the federal government had obtained, by Treaty Number Three with the Ojibwa Indians, the surrender of some 142,445 square kilometres (55,000 square miles) involving much of northwestern Ontario and parts of southeastern Manitoba. The federal government granted timber rights in some of the surrendered land to the St. Catharines Milling and Lumber Company. The government of Ontario objected that, once surrendered by Indians, the land belonged to Ontario, not to Ottawa, and commenced an action to prevent the company from cutting timber on the land. The case eventually reached the Judicial Committee of the Privy Council in London, England, at that time the highest appeal court for Canada. Ruling in favour of Ontario, the court went on to define the nature of Indian rights in land that had not been surrendered to the Crown. In its unanimous decision the Privy Council defined the Indian right as being "a personal and usufructuary right, dependent upon the good will of the sovereign''. This terminology has caused the precedent-bound Canadian court system considerable difficulty because no one is sure what a "personal and usufructuary" right is. Today native land rights are referred to as aboriginal title.

While these early legal decisions established that Indians had rights, albeit undefined rights, to the land, this by no means settled the matter. Indian rights became an important issue after the Second World War. The central question was whether the Indians owned the land, or at least some of the rights in the land that made up Canada. In some parts of Canada, notably the prairies and Ontario, treaties had been signed whereby the Indians gave up their rights in return for parcels of land (now called reserves) and various other payments. However, in the rest of Canada, namely British Columbia, the north, Quebec and the Maritimes, Indians had not (and in most cases still have not) signed treaties or land claims surrendering their land rights.

In 1947 a special joint committee of the Senate and House of Commons recommended the establishment of a commission to settle land claims grievances, similar to the Indian Claims Commission established in the United States in 1946. Nothing happened. A similar recommendation was made again in the early sixties by the same committee. The Diefenbaker government, which had granted Indians the right to vote and had also appointed the first Indian senator, prepared a bill to establish an Indian claims commission but was defeated in 1963 before it had a chance to introduce the bill in the House of Commons.

By the mid-sixties Indian leaders and various support groups began to demand that the government take action on the deplorable Indian situation. With Trudeau coming to power in 1968 promising a "just society", there was reason to believe things would change. The government announced a series of eighteen public meetings to be held across the country to discuss changes to the Indian Act. At the same time several government committees were working in private to come up with a new Indian policy. Their solution was somewhat more drastic than a simple revamping of the Indian Act.

The conclusions reached by these private meetings were adopted by the government and announced on June 25, 1969, when Jean Chrétien, the minister of Indian affairs, introduced the government's White Paper on Indian policy. It proposed doing away with special status for Indians, doing away with treaties and turning responsibility for Indians over to the provinces. Specifically, on aboriginal rights, the paper stated, "These are so general and undefined that it is not realistic to think of them as specific claims capable of remedy…"

Trudeau reaffirmed the government's position in a Vancouver speech on August 8, 1969.

> It's inconceivable I think that in a given society, one section of the society have a treaty with the other section of the society. We must be all equal under the laws and we must not sign treaties amongst ourselves…We can't recognize aboriginal rights because no society can be built on historical "might-have-beens".

Trudeau argued that if the aboriginal rights of Indians were recognized the government would also have to recognize the rights of Quebec, the rights of Acadians who were expelled from Canada and the rights of Japanese Canadians who were relocated during the

Second World War. Ironically, all of these groups have since advanced claims for settlement of past grievances.

Coming from a man who was supposed to be a dedicated civil libertarian and who had promised a "just society", Trudeau's stand was profoundly disturbing to most Indian leaders. His position on their rights was as great a shock to the Indians as his invocation of the War Measures Act was to civil libertarians.

However, while Pierre Trudeau was making his speech, the wheels of justice were also at work and were pointing in a different direction from that in which Trudeau was going. The Nishga Indians had sued for a declaration that their aboriginal or Indian title was still in existence on their lands, which consisted of some 1,000 square miles in northwestern British Columbia.

Many anthropologists believe that the Nishga had the most advanced Indian culture north of Mexico. One of the experts testifying at the trial, which opened in January 1969, said that the Nishga had a highly defined concept of community ownership of land and had developed a system of identifying the boundaries of their land "by natural landmarks with a precision remarkable for people with no surveying equipment". But despite the abundance of evidence heard in support of their claim, the trial judge ultimately ruled against the Nishga and was upheld by the British Columbia Court of Appeal. The case was then taken to the Supreme Court of Canada. There, while technically the Nishga lost, the Court recognized that there was such a thing as aboriginal or Indian title.

Seven Supreme Court judges heard the case. One judge ruled against the Indians on procedural grounds.

Three judges held that there was such a thing as "Indian title", but that it had been extinguished in the 1860s by the unilateral legislative acts of Governor Douglas of the colony of British Columbia, when he issued a series of proclamations authorizing the sale of land to prospective colonists. None of these proclamations mentioned Indian title. However, three judges found that this evidence was sufficient to override Indian title. They also ruled that the government could override Indian rights unilaterally and without consultation.

Three other judges, including Bora Laskin and Emmett Hall, not only recognized Indian title but ruled that the Nishgas' title was still in existence. They said Indian title could only be extinguished by legislative action if the legislation specifically said it was extinguishing Indian title. Furthermore, these judges said there was an assumption in Canadian law that the government would not take away property rights without compensation. These three judges also made it clear that Indian rights meant ownership and not some limited right to use the land.

With six judges of the Supreme Court of Canada recognizing aboriginal or Indian title, the Trudeau government was forced to reassess its position on aboriginal rights. Trudeau himself admitted there might be greater legitimacy to Indian claims than he originally thought. As early as December 1969 the government was showing evidence of its changing position when it appointed a commissioner, Dr. Lloyd Barber, to examine ways of settling treaty and other grievances. The House of Commons Standing Committee on Indian Affairs also endorsed, and pressed the government to adopt, a comprehensive policy of settling native land claims.

Finally, in the summer of 1973 Jean Chrétien announced that the government policy was to recognize and settle documented Indian claims in non-treaty areas. The government announced it would recognize two classes of claims: comprehensive claims based on aboriginal title and specific claims based on promises made but not fulfilled. The federal government also started providing funding (since that time millions of dollars have been provided) for Indian groups to gather evidence to prove their claims. An Office of Native Claims was established in 1974 to evaluate native claims.

While the Nishga were in court suing to prove that they owned their land a classic confrontation was developing in Quebec between developers and native people who wanted to live off the land as their forefathers had done for centuries before. Robert Bourassa came to power in 1970 promising a new economic order that would include thousands of jobs. Central to that promise was the multi-billion-dollar James Bay Hydro Electric development. Bourassa overlooked one thing: some 10,000 Inuit and Cree lived, hunted and trapped in the area where he was planning to build his eighth wonder of the world. The bulldozers came, and the Indians and Inuit went to court to stop them.

Montreal, December 5, 1972. The case began with an application for an injunction (a court order halting the project until such time as it was determined what rights native people had in the land in question). The hearing before Mr. Justice Malouf was supposed to last a few days, but instead it went on until June 21, 1973, and 167 witnesses were called to testify. Malouf took several months to reach his decision and, when it was announced, it shocked Bourassa and the developers.

On November 15, 1973, Mr. Justice Malouf ordered the James Bay Development Corporation, the James Bay Energy Corporation, Hydro-Quebec and twenty-two other contractors to cease work on the project immediately and not to trespass on Indian lands. Allegations were made that the work never did cease, that it went on in spite of the court order. In any event the decision was quickly appealed; the Quebec Court of Appeal lifted the stop order and on further appeal the Supreme Court of Canada upheld the Court of Appeal. The stop order had been lifted, but the question of whether the Indians and Inuit owned the land was still to be determined by the courts. Bourassa, the federal government and the developers, no longer sure of their position, decided to negotiate a settlement with the natives to ensure that the project would not end up in limbo because of a further adverse court decision.

The native people were equally unsure what the final outcome of their litigation would be, and rather than face a protracted legal battle, they decided to accept the offer to negotiate a settlement of their land claims.

A final agreement was signed November 11, 1975. The 455-page document, a mass of legalisms and detail, is still largely misunderstood today. The Inuit and Indians gave up their rights to 400,000 square miles. In return they will get, over the course of the agreement, $225 million ($150 million has now been paid), exclusive control over their village sites, the right to self-government in their communities, certain hunting and fishing rights, and other benefits buried in 455 pages of fine print. Heralded as a precedent-setter when signed, the agreement has done little to improve the situation of the Cree and Inuit in Quebec. A recent government study found most of the Cree in James Bay living in poverty and in unacceptable conditions.

A 1982 federal government report on the James Bay agreement concluded: ''The lack of proper sanitation facilities and poor housing constitutes a continuous health and safety hazard...Some [Inuit schools] do not even provide adequate shelter, let alone a proper learning environment.'' The James Bay people have even been forced to go to court to get action on the agreement.

Five years after the Quebec Superior Court judgement, the Inuit of Baker Lake, Northwest Territories, sued for a court declaration stating that the land in the Baker Lake area (approximately 78,000 square kilometres) was theirs and asking for an order prohibiting the federal and territorial governments from issuing mining leases in the area. They also asked that any companies already exploring for minerals in the area be ordered to stop. The Inuit complained that the prospecting camps and low-flying aircraft were scaring away the caribou, their main food supply. Once again, a classic conflict between development and a centuries-old lifestyle.

After weeks of hearings, including a week's hearings at Baker Lake, the federal court judge defined the four criteria that had to be met before the court would find an aboriginal or Indian title to be valid. Those four criteria were: first, that they (the Indians or Inuit) and their ancestors were members of an organized society; second, that this organized society occupied the specific territory over which they claimed aboriginal title; third, that the occupation was to the exclusion of other organized societies; and finally, that the occupation was an established fact at the time sovereignty was asserted by England. The judge found that the Inuit of Baker Lake met these requirements and declared that they had aboriginal title in some of the lands in question. However, he refused to put a stop to exploration and mining activities in the area.

Not only have the courts recognized Indian land rights, but they have also placed the federal government in a trust position over those rights. The trust responsibility results from the 1985 Supreme Court of Canada decision in the $10-million-dollar case involving the Musqueam Indian band of Vancouver. In January 1958, the Shaughnessy Heights Golf Club entered into a lease for 160 acres belonging to the Musqueam Indian Reserve and located within the City of Vancouver. The lease was for an initial term of fifteen years at $29,000 per year with a right of renewal that made it possible for the club, at its discretion, to rent the property for up to seventy-five years (the club is still in possession of the property). There were ceilings in the lease limiting the rent that could be charged if the club renewed. The lease was negotiated by Indian Affairs officials on behalf of the band. Band members were misled by the officials as to the terms of the lease; they were told the lease was for ten years with the right to renew. Basing their decision on the information they had been given, the Indian band voted 41 to 2 in favour of the lease. Twelve years after the lease was signed, band members were finally successful in getting a copy of the lease. After seeing it they felt they had got a rotten deal and sued the federal government. The trial judge agreed, pointing out that the land was prime residential property and that if it had been developed as residential property it would have produced considerably more income. He awarded the Musqueam Indian band $10 million. The Supreme Court of Canada upheld the trial judge. The Court reaffirmed its earlier recognition of Indian title and said the federal government, by the Indian Act and the reserve system, had taken upon itself the duty of looking after Indian lands. Having undertaken this responsibility it was incumbent on the federal government to get the best deal possible when leasing or selling Indian lands. Not having done so, the federal government was liable in damages to the Musqueam band.

Where do these court decisions leave the state of affairs today? The Canadian courts have clearly recognized the existence of aboriginal title and have enshrined it in Canada's legal system. But the matter does not end there. Indian claims are complex issues; Indians cannot simply walk into a court and say, "Here we are, now give us a court order saying the land is ours." Indian title may have been overruled in some areas by government action. The courts have made it clear that Indian title can be taken away by the federal government. Some judges have said that any government action having to do with land (like the granting of a mining licence) is sufficient to take away Indian title because it is inconsistent with Indian ownership. Other judges have said that the federal government must pass specific laws stating that "Indian title is hereby extinguished", and pay compensation before Indian title can be extinguished. The latter interpretation is consistent with the Royal Proclamation of 1763, which states that lands required for settlement must be purchased. This view would also be consistent with the Canadian notion of property rights — it would be unthinkable for the federal government to take land for an airport without compensating the owners.

Assuming that native people can show that their title has not been extinguished, they still have the burden of proving their title (according to the criteria set out in the Baker Lake case) with evidence that is acceptable in a court of law. Considerable energy is required to find such evidence and, in the final analysis, the judge has to decide whether the evidence proves the case. The Nishga case shows that native people don't always win when they go to court. As a result, native people have often chosen the political route hoping to convince federal leaders of the justice, if not the legality, of their claims.

Land Claims Negotiations Today

The money for research into land claims, litigation and negotiation comes from governments, with the lion's share coming from the federal government. Up to the end of the 1981-82 fiscal year the federal government had granted $16.7 million dollars to Indian groups for land claims negotiation and litigation. Why would Ottawa give money so that it could be dragged into court or have to negotiate multi-million-dollar land claims settlements? To some extent this largesse is prompted by a genuine concern for justice, but probably more than one politician sees this as a way of buying off the Indians.

Since James Bay, the number of comprehensive claims advanced totals over forty, and new claims are advanced almost every year. However, since the federal government announced its comprehensive land claims policy in 1973 only one claim has been settled (aside from the James-Bay-related Northeastern Quebec Agreement of 1978), that of the Inuvialuit of the western Arctic, in 1984. Under that agreement the 2,500 Inuvialet will receive approximately $150 million, to be paid over thirteen years. In addition they were given title to 90,000 square kilometres of land, an area about one and a half times the size of Nova Scotia. They were also given the mineral rights on 13,000 of 90,000 square kilometres. In return they surrendered all their rights to about 344,000 square kilometres.

A number of specific claims, resulting from specific government promises made in the past, have also been settled. These generally have involved small parcels of land and have affected few people. Specific claims have to date numbered close to 300.

While progress has been made on other comprehensive claims the question arises: why do land claims take so long to settle? There are many reasons, arising from the concerns of both native groups and the government. Many native groups are reluctant to sign away their rights in a one-shot deal. Rather than extinguishment of their rights they propose a sharing of the land. In short, rather than selling their rights, they propose a long-term lease. They take this position because they feel no lump-sum payment, however large, can ever totally compensate for land that is being given up for ever and ever. Therefore, Indian leaders have argued, ''Let's keep our aboriginal title and simply share the land with other Canadians in return for adequate compensation.'' This would mean a guaranteed income for Indians in perpetuity and would also allow the lease to be changed if at some future time the Indians felt they had got a bad deal. To date the federal government has insisted that Indians surrender their rights once and for all.

There are other reasons why negotiations have moved slowly. Indian concepts of time are very different from those of non-native society. Non-natives think in terms of deadlines and of deals being completed as soon as possible. Indians have not been as concerned with firm deadlines. The land has been around for a long time and they want to make sure they get a good deal before relinquishing it. Historically, most treaties and land deals signed have been entered into and negotiated on the government's timetable. Be it to open up the prairies or build the James Bay Hydro Electric development, the government has wanted to get on with a project or settlement and has dictated the pace of negotiation. Indians with outstanding land claims look at their brethren from the prairies, Ontario and James Bay. They see that the lot of Indians who have signed treaties is not a happy one. Poverty, alcoholism and unemployment are rampant. It is not surprising that Canada's native people are not waiting with pens poised to sign land claims agreements. They want to try to avoid their brethren's problems.

There are also native groups who would prefer never to surrender their aboriginal rights. Even the idea of leasing their land for development is unsatisfactory to them. However, they realize that in the past development has often proceeded without the consent of native people, and they fear that if they refuse to discuss the surrender of their aboriginal title, development will simply proceed without their consent. Essentially, the means for blocking development are physical blockade and the courts. Neither route guarantees success. Therefore, a realistic assessment of the facts forces many native groups, otherwise opposed to surrendering their title, to hope for the best possible settlement, some say in the pace and type of development that will occur on their lands, and their fair share of the economic benefits associated with development. They also hope that through negotiations they can save some remote areas from development so that those of their people who so choose can pursue a traditional hunting lifestyle.

With all of these factors in mind, Indian negotiators have preferred to move slowly and cautiously.

On the government's side are two factors which have given rise to delay. First, not every Canadian is convinced that land claims need to be settled; and second, there is cost. With each succeeding year new claims are being documented. Each new claim means more money; coupled with inflation this means that the bill for land claims increases every year. A 1963 estimate of the cost of known land claims was $17.4 million. Ten years later, the cash settlement in the James Bay agreement alone amounted to $225 million, not including the cost of various services that the federal and Quebec governments have agreed to provide to the Cree and Inuit. The sum of all land claims today probably amounts to billions of dollars. With the federal deficit still growing, there is certainly concern in some circles about cost. Land claims costs have given fuel to opponents who echo Trudeau's question why one segment of society should have to make a deal with another segment. However, the Indians do have one trump card: if politicians remain too reluctant there is always the option of going to court. Aboriginal title has been recognized by the courts and history has shown that Indians are likely to win some of their cases. And they can always lobby in the international forum using such avenues as the United Nations.

The federal government has also had in place a policy of negotiating no more than six claims at any one time. This has meant that many claims are on hold.

In July 1985, Indian Affairs Minister David Crombie appointed a task force to review the federal government's policies regarding comprehensive claims. The report, released in early 1986, recommended a change in policy. It suggested that the multi-million-dollar one-time settlement should be abandoned in favour of

long-term sharing arrangements. It recommended that
land-use agreements should encourage self-government, economic self-sufficiency, and cultural preser-
vation. And it suggested that extinguishment of Indian
title was not necessary in every case. If extinguishment
was needed, the report argued against unilateral extinguishment.

Another government report, the Nielsen study on
government spending released around the same time,
recommended that comprehensive land claims negotiations be put on hold.

Assuming that a land claim is accepted by the
government (and many have been) the difficult question arises of how to determine the compensation to
be paid. Should it be an outright cash payment, should
it be cash over a period of time, should it involve land
reserved exclusively for native people, should it be a
percentage of income earned from the land, should it
be a combination of land and money, or should it
include other benefits as well? And as of what date
should the compensation be determined? Should the
Indians get what the land was worth when the colo-
nizers took over the land, plus interest, or should it
be priced at today's market value? If it is to be valued
at today's prices, should Indians be compensated for
market value (including improvements) or for raw land?
The federal government has prepared some general
guidelines for determining compensation. However,
these are guidelines and in the end compensation will
be dependent upon the skills, will and determination
that each side brings to the negotiating table.

The state of New South Wales in Australia has come
up with a novel way of paying for land claim settlements. It imposes a land tax on the sale of all Crown
land to finance land claim settlements.

Land claims are a massive undertaking. It will likely take another twenty or thirty years before all land claims negotiations are completed. The pace of negotiations will certainly be influenced by the pace of economic development. If economic pressure increases to develop resources in remoter, more isolated areas of Canada, then so will the pressure to settle land claims increase. Resource development will bring pressure to bear on both sides — the government anxious to proceed with development without hindrance from native claims, and native people, fearing that development will proceed whether they like it or not, determined that therefore they will not settle for anything less than the best deal possible.

3
National Indian Policy

June 11, 1981. Four hundred heavily armed police-men, backed with bulldozers, helicopters and an assortment of other vehicles, approached an unsuspecting community in the hour before dawn. This was not a police-backed coup in some banana republic, but the Quebec Provincial Police enforcing fisheries regulations on the Restigouche Indian reserve near the Quebec-New Brunswick border. Several days before, Quebec Fisheries Minister Lucien Lessard warned the Micmacs of Restigouche to remove their nets from the Restigouche River. The Micmacs replied that it was their aboriginal right (a right that they had always had and had never given up) to catch salmon. The pre-dawn raid resulted in the seizure of some 250 kilograms of salmon and more than seventy-five nets.

Nine days later a second police raid took place, again ostensibly to enforce fisheries regulations. Police fired tear gas and blocked the bridge linking the reserve with Campbellton, New Brunswick. In turn, the Micmacs blocked the four roads leading into the reserve with their vehicles.

Fortunately, several hours later, Canada's 1981 "Salmon War" ended without violence when police withdrew from the reserve boundaries. Eventually, Quebec and the Micmacs were able to reach an understanding regarding fishing rights. During this "war", the federal government did nothing, despite its constitutional responsibility for Indians.

Constitutional Responsibility for Native People

When the colonies — the Canadas, New Brunswick and Nova Scotia — decided to federate in 1867, there was almost no discussion as to which level of government should be responsible for Indians. The assumption was that it should be the federal level, since provinces were taking on responsibility for local matters while the federal government was assuming many of the responsibilities which London had handled previously.

The country's hoped-for future also suggested that Indian matters should be handled by Ottawa. The Fathers of Confederation envisaged Canada stretching from sea to sea, with the responsibility for exploring the west and north resting with the federal government. The 1867 British North America Act specifically made provision for the admission of new colonies into the federation, including the Northwest Territories and Rupert's Land. Expansion to the north and west would bring the Indian question to a head in areas for which only the federal government could assume the responsibility.

While primary responsibility for Indians stayed with the federal level, today the provinces have some obligations to their native populations. Sometimes the provinces have tried to evade even their limited responsibility; sometimes they have tried to assume wider authority. Similarly, the federal government has on occasion tried to pass off its duties to the provinces. The constitutional wrangling has added to the difficulties of formulating a uniform national policy on native matters.

Some commentators suggested that the 1981 "Salmon War" had nothing to do with the enforcement of Quebec fisheries regulations but represented yet another struggle between Quebec and Ottawa. This would not be the first or the last time that native people have been pawns in a federal-provincial struggle. The struggle at times has not been over power, but rather a contest in which the goal for both sides is to escape financial responsibility for Indians — in short the reverse of the normal power situation.

Constitutional problems arise because, in Canadian federalism, lines of jurisdiction are not always clear. While the constitution says that "Indians and lands reserved for Indians" are a federal responsibility, the courts have always held that Indians are citizens of the province that they live in and are therefore subject to the same provincial laws, and entitled to the same benefits, as anyone else, unless those laws interfere with some federal program or law dealing with Indians.

To add to the confusion, the federal government enacted legislation in 1951 making provincial laws applicable to Indians unless such laws conflicted with a treaty or federal law. Since then there have been thousands of court cases dealing with the application of provincial laws to Indians and their reserves. The jurisdictional questions on which the courts have had to rule have been far more diverse than even the most creative legal mind might have imagined: do Indians have to pay provincial sales tax; do they have to pay sales tax if the dealer brings a car to the reserve and the deal is signed there; do provincial traffic laws apply on the reserve; are Indians subject to the same hunting laws as other people; and when an Indian couple breaks up, can a provincial court order that the wife has the absolute right to remain in the reserve house?

A related issue is the question of who is legally an Indian under the constitution and therefore qualifies as a federal responsibility. Does it only include Indian-Act Indians, or does it include Métis and other people of native ancestry who do not fall under the Indian Act? Canada's Métis argue that they too are part of the federal government's constitutional responsibility, but Ottawa has rejected this interpretation. (However, during the 1985 Constitutional Conference on Aboriginal Rights Prime Minister Mulroney agreed to begin negotiations with the Métis and non-status Indians on the definition of their rights.)

Several decades earlier a similar debate arose regarding the Inuit. In the 1930s the federal and Quebec governments differed over responsibility for social programs for the Inuit in northern Quebec. The Supreme Court of Canada decided in 1939 that the Inuit were a federal responsibility, even outside the northern territories.

Because the constitution says that Indians are a federal responsibility the Indian community has often objected to having to deal with the provinces regarding their rights. Thus on more than one occasion before, during and after the constitutional conferences on aboriginal rights held in the last few years Indians have objected to the presence of provinces at the constitutional table.

Some Indian leaders even go so far as to argue that all their dealings should be with the Queen, because treaties were signed (in those areas of Canada where treaties have been signed) between them and the Queen. During the fight over Canada's constitution, in the late 1970s and early 1980s, several Canadian Indian groups tried to get a court declaration in England saying that the federal government could not interfere with their rights because of their special relationship with the Queen. The English courts rejected this argument.

Constitutional difficulties have certainly complicated the formation of policies regarding native people. However, in fairness, the task was made even more difficult by the fact that the policies of the colonial governments of pre-Confederation Canada were sometimes at odds, and Ottawa inherited those contradictions. The foundation for early colonial policies was laid by England.

Early British Policies

Officially, the British transferred responsibility for Indians to the United Province of Canada in 1860; however, even before then control over Indian matters was gradually being passed to the Canadas (Upper and Lower Canada, today Quebec and Ontario) and to the colonies of Nova Scotia and New Brunswick. The transfer took place for many reasons, amongst others that the British were not anxious to pay for Indian lands, which by their Royal Proclamation of 1763 they had to buy from the Indians in order to make them available for settlement. It was the colonies that would benefit from settlement, and so therefore, the British reasoned, the colonists should be responsible for the acquisition of lands.

Besides the requirement that land needed for settlement had to be purchased from the Indians, another long-standing theme of British policy was the need, in the words of colonial administrators, "to protect these helpless children", so that they could eventually reach adulthood — that is, become full citizens. To a large extent this philosophy was continued by many of Britain's North American colonies, though its application led some of the colonies to quite different policy positions.

While the British had developed these policy guidelines it was left to colonial administrators to put them into effect, and the many gaps — areas not covered by British policy — were left to the colonies to fill.

The colony where British policy was least noticeable was probably Quebec. Prior to the capitulation of Quebec to England in 1760, Quebec colonial authorities paid little attention to Indian matters. While French colonial officials made alliances with the Indians to fight and harass the British, the education and welfare of Indians were left to various religious orders in the Catholic Church; the Jesuits were the most active. The orders were mostly concerned with converting Indians to Christianity.

When the British conquered Quebec, the church's responsibilities were not changed. In fact, land granted to the church to be used for the benefit of Indians specifically remained church property even after British conquest.

Although the English, unlike the French, tried to develop an policy for dealing with aboriginal people, and certainly gave greater recognition to Indian rights than other European powers had done, things in colonial Canada did not always go smoothly. Confusion, conflict and outright dishonesty were often the order of the day, whether one spoke of Upper Canada, which in the 1840s was joined with Quebec to form Canada, the maritime colonies of Nova Scotia and New Brunswick, or the colony of British Columbia. And in 1867 the federal government inherited this confusion.

Originally the British Imperial War Department took responsibility for Indians, because whether the British were fighting the French or the Americans, Indians were very much a part of any war effort (whether as allies or enemies). With the establishment of peace in

North America (the last war was fought in 1812-14 with the Americans) the British became less interested in Indian matters and began turning them over to the colonial governments, which were not always anxious to take on this responsibility and often did not know what to do. However, the transfer continued, so that by the time Confederation occurred the English were totally out of the Indian business.

Land policies are a good example of the kind of confusion that ensued. While official policy required that lands had to be purchased from Indians, and prohibited squatting or trespassing on Indian lands, the reality was often in direct contravention of official policy. Squatting and trespassing on Indian lands were everyday occurrences. To many of the colonists it seemed a shame for all that land to go unused, to sit there idle, often with no sign of its Indian inhabitants. They could see no reason for not helping themselves to it. Occasionally, Indians would complain about this; sometimes a colonial legislature would even pass laws prohibiting settlers from taking Indian lands. However, in colonies that at the time had few resources, the enforcement of such laws did not rate a high priority. To enforce such laws would literally mean sending enforcement officers out in the woods to evict a squatter and sometimes, to solve the problem, legislation would be passed validating the title of the squatter, or at least allowing him to buy the land.

The English land policy created a further difficulty: who was to pay for Indian land? England had reservations about paying for Indian lands that would then be available for colonials. The colonials, on the other hand, assumed it was an English responsibility.

The money issue is one reason why native land claims were never settled in British Columbia. In the late 1850s and early 1860s, Governor Douglas of British Columbia was most anxious to settle with the Indians but lacked the money. The Colonial Office replied that this was a local matter and that it could hardly be expected that the British taxpayer should be burdened with having to pay for colonial expansion. Douglas, finding himself with no money, proceeded to open up British Columbia for settlement without bothering to buy Indian lands. As a result, the issue of native land rights in British Columbia is still unresolved.

One concept developed in Upper Canada for dealing with the cost issue was to use income from the sale of land to pay off the Indians. Land was obtained from the Indians in return for a guaranteed annual payment. The land would be sold to a settler who would pay in annual instalments, and these would provide the income with which to pay the Indians. This concept was developed as a way of preventing a drain on the public treasury.

A modified version of this concept was utilized on the prairies when the numbered treaties were signed. Thus today, on the prairies, there are still Treaty days, when a federal official sitting under the Queen's portrait and flanked by a Mountie in a scarlet tunic hands out the treaty money (five dollars under most treaties) to each treaty Indian. This treaty payment represents yet another instalment on the agreement wherein Indians sold their lands.

Another issue that was left to the colonies was the question of the Indian's place in society; there had to be an official policy on this. It apparently never occurred to colonial administrators that perhaps the best policy might be to leave the Indian alone. Suggestions ranged from extermination to integration. The problem with the latter was that the English settlers, unlike their

French or Spanish counterparts, were reluctant to inter-marry. The official policy finally adopted by the English Colonial Office was civilization. The chief instrument by which this was to be achieved was the reserve: Indians would be settled on reserves, where they would be taught trades and agricultural skills, and where their children could go to school and be Christianized.

In Ontario and on the prairies, reserves were often established in conjunction with the signing of a treaty. As part of the treaty settlement, Indians were promised that certain lands would be set aside for them. Reserves in other parts of Canada were simply established by governments unilaterally setting aside land for Indians. It very quickly became evident that the reserve policy was not achieving its goal. Rather than becoming civilized, the Indians on reserves were becoming more and more dependent on public assistance. The contra-diction of the policy never struck the policy-makers: if you segregate a segment of the population on reserves, away from the mainstream of society, it will be virtually impossible to integrate the population into the society at large.

Today, of course, the policy is irreversible. Meagre though the allotments are, Indian reserves are viewed by Indian people as their homeland, a place where they can preserve Indian culture and language. Indian reserves also provide a territorial base in which Indians can govern themselves.

To the policy-makers of the time it was self-evident that there could be no question of allowing the Indians — ''unlettered savages'' — to decide what would happen on their reserves, and so they took it upon themselves to make the rules. All of the colonies passed legislation to deal with reserve land. The titles of the laws passed tell the story of how colonial legislatures viewed the Indians' ability to manage their own affairs — An Act to provide for the Instruction and Permanent Settlement of the Indians (Nova Scotia, 1842), An Act to regulate the management and disposal of the Indian Reserves (New Brunswick, 1844), An Act to encourage the gradual civilization of the Indians in this Province, and to amend the laws respecting Indians (United Canadas, Ontario and Quebec, 1857). The assumption behind these early colonial acts, that Indians are incapable of regulating their own affairs, was carried forward into the Indian Act, first passed by the federal Parliament in 1876. That policy remained for the greater part of the twentieth century.

Native Policy in the Confederation Era

Confederation did not mean a change in Indian policy in Canada. In fact, the federal government inherited many of the contradictions in colonial policies, some of which it has never been able to resolve. The official policy — that lands required for settlement had to be bought from the Indians — was continued. It was for this reason that the new Dominion entered into various treaties with the Indians in northwestern Ontario and on the prairies. The concept of reserves was also continued, as was the idea that until the Indian was civilized, he would be incapable of handling his own affairs.

One aspect of the "civilization" process was the attempt to keep Indians away from the evils of white society, and particularly, away from alcohol. Almost from the day the Europeans arrived in the Americas the attempt to control alcohol use by Indians was a major preoccupation of policy-makers and church leaders. Of course, matters were not helped by the fact that other Europeans were far less averse to providing the Indians with alcohol. Even in the early French days, alcohol was a problem. In the early 1700s, the Oka reserve in Quebec was relocated to increase the distance between it and Montreal, where alcohol was so easily available. British colonial administrators banned or severely restricted alcohol consumption by Indians and on Indian lands. The first legislative measure was in 1835, when Upper Canada passed a bill prohibiting the sale, barter, exchange or gift of alcohol to any Indian man, woman or child.

Eyewitness accounts tell the story of the sad state to which the Indians had been reduced by alcohol. One Alfred Domett passed through Brantford on his tour of Upper Canada in the 1830s; he reported that his carriage "narrowly escaped running over some drunken Indians who were lying in the muddy road." The Reverend John Carroll recalled the state of the Mississauga Indians in the 1860s: "They were drunkards to a man — their women totally divorced of virtue — and the whole of them sunk in poverty and filth beyond expression. At the time of their receiving their annuities and presents...a Bacchanalian revel took place, which usually lasted days, and issued in squandering every copper of money and selling or pawning every article they had received for the deadly 'firewater'." Another observer, John Howison, described what followed the annual distribution of payments in the 1820s to the Indians around Lake Erie: "The Indians spent all the money they received in this way upon spirits; hence drunkenness ensues — fatal combats take place — and shocking scenes of outrage, intoxication, and depravity, continue until the actors are stripped of all they possess."

While the official policy, influenced by various Protestant churches and the temperance movement, was to control or severely restrict alcohol use by Indians, the reality was often very different. This was not simply because the Indians wanted alcohol but rather because drinking in the Canadian colonies was a widespread social problem (as it was in England and Europe during the eighteenth and nineteenth centuries). Professor F.L. Barron writing about *Alcoholism, Indians, and the Anti-Drink Cause in the Protestant Indian Missions of Upper Canada 1822-1850* (which appeared in the book *As Long as the Sun Shines and Water Flows*) put things in perspective by stating that in the year 1850, in Upper Canada alone, there were forty-nine breweries, which produced in excess of 3.4 million litres of beer; there were 100 distilleries whose annual output was 13.5 million litres of hard liquor (when whisky was 50 per cent stronger than it is today); and the colony imported 1.8 million litres of wine and hard liquor. All of this for a population of less than one million. By the 1870s Toronto had over 500 saloons, a quart of beer cost less than a newspaper and for the price of a live show you could buy a gallon or two of whisky. Not surprisingly, the Indians got caught up in this debauchery.

The new Dominion continued the policy of trying to restrict the availability of alcohol to Indians, and the legacy of this policy is still with us today. Until 1985 there were special provisions in the Indian Act controlling use of liquor on reserves. The 1985 changes to the Indian Act gave band councils greater control over alcohol use on reserves. And it was well into the 1950s and 1960s before Indians gained the right to drink in bars.

The Opening of the West

After Confederation, the new Dominion proceeded expeditiously on the alcohol problem in the west, with the idea of nipping it in the bud. In the 1860s gun-toting whisky traders began moving north from Montana. In part they were running away from attempts to bring law and order to the western United States, but they also saw the Canadian west as a place where they could make an easy profit. Several "whisky forts" were established, the most notorious being the appropriately named Fort Whoop-Up, near Lethbridge, Alberta. It was reported in the Montana press that Whoop-Up country was inhabited by persons whose sole occupation is "trading whisky to Indians, and as they are in British America no notice will be taken of their crimes by the United States authorities." In the early 1870s the Canadian government sent two expeditions to tour the area and report on the state of law and order. They reported that murder and mayhem were the order of the day. The federal government realized that if this violence were allowed to continue unabated it would have serious implications for the settlement of the west. The answer was the creation of the North-West Mounted Police in 1873. However, before the force could be dispatched a major incident occurred, which forced the federal government to move even faster than it had anticipated.

A number of American wolf hunters were visiting a trading post in the Cypress Hills area (in south-western Saskatchewan) and were told by one of the traders that he suspected his horse had been stolen by Assiniboine Indians camped nearby. After the consumption of generous quantities of alcohol the hunters decided the Indians should be taught a lesson.

Forty lodges of peaceful Assiniboines were attacked; sixteen men, women and children were killed and their bodies mutilated beyond recognition.

The Cypress Hill Massacre forced the federal government to speed up the dispatch of the North-West Mounted Police. One of their first duties was to bring the hunters to justice. The federal government was most anxious to placate the Indians by assuring them that settlement of the west would proceed in a peaceful manner and that the perpetrators of the massacre would be brought to justice.

In another measure meant to control lawlessness, the federal government declared all of the west dry; this was aimed at whisky traders and it was hoped that it would ensure some peace and stability in Indian communities. Pierre Berton, in his book *The Last Spike* points out that this measure also had a salutary effect on the construction of the transcontinental railway. According to Berton, one reason why the railway was completed in four years (1881-85) was that, without alcohol, there was a sober and efficient work force to see that the job got done.

The bringing of law and order was but one step in the process of achieving the "national dream" of a Canada stretching from sea to sea, its two coasts linked by a railway that crossed the country from the Atlantic to the Pacific. The dream also involved the settling of the west, and its opening up as a supplier of raw materials for the centrally located manufacturing industries. The west was also to be a captive market for eastern manufactured goods. Both before and in the early days after Confederation there was considerable debate about the national dream — was it feasible to think of a country stretching right across the American continent? Did the small eastern colonies have the resources and manpower to open up the west, and did the west have any potential?

At the time of Confederation all of the west, with the exception of Vancouver Island and parts of the lower mainland of British Columbia (which was a separate colony), was owned by the Hudson's Bay Company. The company had obtained the territory by Royal Charter in 1670. Much of northern Ontario and Quebec also belonged to the company. The company was more than a trading company, it was also the government for the whole territory. Thus it was the company's responsibility to look after Indian matters in its territories. The Company's Indian policy was one of benign neglect. The Indians were seen as suppliers of furs or as middlemen in dealings with other Indians. Little attention was paid to such matters as education or civilization of the Indians.

In order for the dream of a nation to become reality it was necessary to acquire the land held by the Hudson's Bay Company. This became the first order of business for the young Dominion. On July 15, 1870, Rupert's Land and the North-Western Territory were transferred to the Dominion of Canada. In accepting Rupert's Land (generally the land draining into Hudson Bay) the federal government agreed that:

> Any claims of Indians to compensation for lands required for purposes of settlement shall be disposed of by the Canadian government in communication with the Imperial Government; and the Company shall be relieved of all responsibility in respect of them.

In accepting the North-Western Territory Canada agreed that:

...upon the transference of the territories in question to the Canadian government, the claims of Indian tribes to compensation for lands required for purposes of settlement will be considered and settled in conformity with the equitable principles which have uniformly governed the British Crown in its dealings with the aborigines.

However, in negotiating this transfer none of the Indian or Métis inhabitants of the west were consulted. The proposed transfer caused considerable anxiety amongst the Métis community in the Red River Valley; they feared that their land, their way of life and their culture would be destroyed. In order to protect themselves they formed their own government and on December 8, 1869, declared themselves to be an independent nation, with Louis Riel as president.

Once the west was admitted into Canada developments proceeded at a rapid pace. From the Indian point of view at too rapid a pace. In southern Ontario and Quebec, as well as in the Maritimes, Indians had had at least a century, sometimes more, to adapt to the coming of the Europeans. In the west the Indians had to make the adjustment in a matter of twenty or thirty years — a dramatic case of "world reversal".

In the 1840s and 1850s Indians were still living a traditional lifestyle in western Canada. The buffalo was central to their existence. Paul Kane, an artist from York (now Toronto), was the first to make pictorial representations of life on the plains. On one of his sketching trips, in the late 1840s, he observed that "...the whole of the three days that it took us to reach Edmonton House, we saw nothing else but these animals [buffalo] covering the plains as far as the eye could reach, and so numerous were they, that at times they impeded our progress, filling the air with dust almost to suffocation.''

By the 1870s the buffalo were gone and starvation was rampant amongst Indians, as was smallpox. At least one historian alleges that the federal government deliberately refused to provide food for the starving Indians, in order to beat them into submission. It was not only hunger and disease that battered the Indians. After signing treaties, they were put on reserves, railways were built across their traditional hunting lands, and surveyors began to parcel out land on which they had recently roamed freely. On top of this, there was a whole new set of rules for living, which were enforced by the police. All of this change within a lifetime was more than most Indians could cope with. The effects of this ''world reversal'' are still with us today.

While Indians in Canada died of disease and starvation, few died, as they did in the United States, from army bullets. Indian wars, or more correctly, massacres of Indians by the American army, were the order of the day when the American west was opened up. As late as 1890 the American army killed 153 Sioux and injured scores more in a massacre at Wounded Knee, South Dakota.

Of course, there were confrontations between whites and Indians in the opening of the Canadian west but few ended with bullets. In part that may have been because rather than having the cavalry riding around, Canada had the North-West Mounted Police, who usually travelled in small numbers and thus depended upon diplomacy rather than guns for survival.

Thus, in the opening of the west, the government's policy on Indians reached full fruition. Lands required for settlement were purchased from the Indians as required under the Royal Proclamation of 1763. Policy enforcement was one of benevolent paternalism; while land had to be paid for, there was pressure on the Indians to give up their land so that development could proceed. And somewhere in that policy was the hope that somehow (no one was sure how) the Indian could be civilized and assimilated into the mainstream of Canadian society.

Hunting and Fishing Protected on the Prairies

As the west was settled, Manitoba was expanded, and Alberta and Saskatchewan were formed in 1905. In the case of each of these three prairie provinces the federal government retained control of the natural resources (minerals, timber lands and Crown land). It was only in 1930 that the federal government transferred control over natural resources to the three provinces. A separate agreement was signed with each province. Each of those agreements contained an important guarantee of Indian hunting rights. That guarantee, in the form of a separate paragraph in the agreement, was a recognition by the Canadian government and the prairie provinces that Indians have special hunting rights and that many of them are dependent on hunting for food. The paragraph, regarded by many prairie Indians as their charter of hunting rights, provides:

> In order to secure to the Indians of the Province the continuance of the supply of game and fish for their support and subsistence, Canada agrees that the laws respecting game in force in the Province from time to time shall apply to the Indians within the boundaries thereof, provided, however, that the said Indians shall have the right, which the province hereby assures to them, of hunting, trapping and fishing game and fish

for food at all seasons of the year on all unoccupied Crown lands and on any other lands to which the said Indians may have a right of access.

This paragraph was a restricted restatement of the treaty hunting rights Indians already had: an unlimited right to hunt on any land not required for settlement. The above paragraph, however, defined that "unlimited" right more narrowly as the right to hunt only when he was hunting for food. Since the signing of these agreements provincial governments on the prairies have often made a concerted effort to limit Indian hunting rights by actively enforcing provincial game laws. The thousands of court cases that have resulted have given rise to the justifiable suspicion that the provinces are not especially concerned about living up to their commitments. Had the governments of the day realized the amount of legal controversy this paragraph would give rise to they probably would not have included it.

There is probably no area of native rights which is as contentious as the issue of hunting rights. Indians are often accused of over-hunting and seriously jeopardizing the supply of wildlife. Such accusations have been levelled by conservation officers, wildlife groups and other citizens. One letter-writer to a daily newspaper put it this way "...I know the worst place to look for wildlife is on or near an Indian Reserve. Often residents feel it is their right to hunt and fish wherever, and however, they choose, in total disregard of laws designed to protect these resources...If Aboriginal self-government is to include taking over fisheries and wildlife management, I am concerned. Can aboriginals be trusted with this task?"

Indians argue that if there is any depletion of game it is the direct result of overhunting by sports hunters and also the destruction of natural habitat on which game sustains itself. They point out that many Indian people still live at the poverty level and that hunting is necessary to their survival. They argue that someone who is dependent upon wildlife for sustenance is not going to destroy his/her way of life. There was no problem with game shortage until Europeans came to the Americas. They point to that fact that under Indian management there never was any shortage of buffalo on the prairies. Indian people argue that their right to live off the land by hunting was guaranteed by the Royal Proclamation of 1763, by subsequent treaties and finally by the natural resources transfer agreements.

The issue of hunting rights, and in particular the hunting paragraph of the Natural Resources Transfer Agreements, has resulted in thousands of court cases. While this judicial activity has been a boon to the legal system it has left considerable confusion as to exactly what hunting rights Indian people have. On the prairies, many of the court cases have attempted to define the hunting provision of the Natural Resources Transfer Agreement.

Essentially, the thrust of that paragraph as interpreted by the courts is that Indians do not have to observe provincial game laws and are not restricted to hunting seasons or limits, if they are hunting for food. The courts have also said that Indians are not restricted in the manner of hunting, unless it presents a danger to the public. Thus, the courts have ruled that Indians may use spotlights and hunt at night if they are hunting for food; they may also use vehicles to assist in the hunt. However, they are not exempt from safety rules. Thus a group of Indians who were hunting at night with spotlights and high-powered rifles in the vicinity of occupied farm buildings were found guilty of hunting without due regard for the safety of others. On the other hand, some courts have ruled that a loaded rifle in a vehicle is not an inherently dangerous practice. What is and what is not a dangerous practice is something the courts have to decide in each individual case. Of course, whether something gets to court at all depends in the first instance on the investigating conservation officer or police officer. If he or she lays no charges, then the matter goes no further.

By the hunting paragraph, Indians are only exempted from provincial law if they are using safe practices and are hunting for food on unoccupied Crown land or other land to which they have a right of access. There have been numerous court cases, including several cases heard by the Supreme Court of Canada, that have tried to define "unoccupied Crown lands". Roads and lands used for resource or recreation development are deemed to be occupied; therefore, Indians are not exempt from the application of game laws in such areas. There is some uncertainty regarding the status of game preserves and conservation areas.

By virtue of the hunting paragraph of the Natural Resources Transfer Agreement Indians also have a right to hunt anywhere that the general public has hunting rights. On this basis, the Supreme Court of Canada has held that, although the Saskatchewan government allows only a limited season in wildlife management units, Indians have the right to hunt there all year round. Similarly Indians may hunt on private lands, without having to obey provincial game laws, in those provinces where the general public has the right to hunt on private lands.

The paragraph does not exempt them from the application of federal hunting laws, the most important being the Migratory Birds Convention Act, dealing with all migratory birds including ducks and geese. The Supreme Court of Canada has ruled that neither the hunting guarantees in the treaties nor the hunting paragraph in the Natural Resources Transfer Agreement exempt Indians from the application of the Migratory Birds Convention Act.

Paul Daniels of the Chemahawin Indian Reserve near The Pas, Manitoba was charged with having shot a duck out of season on July 4, 1964. His case went all the way to the Supreme Court of Canada. He argued that the charge was not valid because his right to hunt for food was guaranteed by the Natural Resources Transfer Agreement. The court said (in a five/four split) that the Migratory Birds Convention Act dated from 1917 while the Natural Resources Agreement only dated from 1929; therefore that Agreement should be read as being subject to the Act. Thus Indians hunting for ducks or geese are subject to many of the same rules as any other Canadians. Similarly, they are not exempted from the rules of the federal Fisheries Act.

Indian hunting and fishing rights in other parts of Canada (outside the prairies) depend upon whether their claims are supported by treaties that protect those rights.

The Indian position on the matter of hunting and trapping rights has been that game management should be turned over to aboriginal people themselves, especially on Indian lands. Hunting and fishing rights are aboriginal rights, guaranteed by treaty and (on the prairies) by the Natural Resources Transfer Agreements, the Indians say. The government view, on the other hand, has usually been that a concession (or a gift) is being made to the Indians. That view was most strongly stated in 1891 by Charles Tupper, federal minister of fisheries, when he instructed Indian agents to:

> use all their influence to make Indians under their supervision understand that in extending to them the valuable privilege they now enjoy of taking fish for their own use, whenever and howsoever they choose, such permission is not to be considered as a right, but as an act of grace, which may be withdrawn at any time...

In other words, Indians see their right to hunt and fish as their inheritance; governments see it as a gift in their power to bestow or take away.

Canada's Last Frontier: The North

Nowhere is the conflict sharper than on Canada's last frontier. Many aboriginal people in the north are dependent on hunting and trapping as a way of existence. It is estimated that some 56,000 Indians, Inuit and Métis still trap for a living. These trappers now face a new threat, in addition to opposition from government policy-makers: various international animal rights organizations, such as Greenpeace and the International Fund for Animal Welfare, have been pushing for a European boycott of Canadian furs, because Canadian trappers use leghold traps (though the protest has died down and some organizations are reconsidering their position after strong protests from native groups). If such a boycott were successful it would virtually destroy the livelihood of these 56,000 people. An aboriginal spokesperson, Miriam McNab, writing in the *Sheaf*, a student newspaper at the University of Saskatchewan, summed up the controversy as follows:

The issue described here is a complex multi-faceted one, which boils down to a basic difference in philosophy between the Aboriginal peoples who live on the land, and the non-Aboriginal urban dwellers, so far removed from their own hunter-gatherer beginnings. The latter group feels that mankind has upset the balance of Nature and has no right to continue to be a predator using modern technology.

Aboriginal peoples know that this is not so. We know that predation by man is necessary and that wildlife management and sustained yield practices do not threaten the natural balance, but ensure it.

The conflict between the traditional native way of life and the urban-based technological society of most Canadians is likely to increase as Canada's last frontier, the north, is opened up. The Canadian north became a part of Canada in 1870, when it was bought from the Hudson's Bay Company, along with western Canada, but for decades it suffered from benign neglect by the federal government. Except for a brief time during the Yukon gold rush of the late 1890s, most Canadians saw the north as a barren land with little potential. This was perfectly fine for the aboriginal inhabitants of that area — it meant that they were largely left to determine their own lifestyle and take only what they needed from southern society.

The first white settlement to have an impact on northern peoples came in the 1920s, after the Hudson's Bay Company had established trading posts through most of the north, and while the churches were busy establishing missions. During this same period, and in particular between the two world wars, the RCMP was establishing itself across the north. However, while alien laws, religions and commerce had come to the north, northern peoples continued their traditional lives of hunting and fishing. The incursion on their lives was relatively minor.

The Second World War changed that. The north took on a new strategic importance. It was feared that Alaska might be invaded by the Japanese; for defence, the Alaska highway was built across the southern Yukon. Whitehorse became a distribution centre for manpower and materials and its population rose almost overnight from about 700 to 40,000. New communities sprang up along the highway; of the eight Yukon communities along the Alaska highway, four came into existence as a result of its being built. Other Yukon towns and villages, not along the highway, declined in population or in some cases ceased to exist. Indian and Métis people began moving to communities along the highway. Some of them gave up their traditional way of life and tried to adapt to the new ways. Of these, some failed, and people who had been self-sufficient hunters and trappers ended up as welfare wards, increasingly dependent on alcohol.

The war had other impacts on northern life. The fur market collapsed, and at the same time the caribou herds began to decline dramatically. Starvation became a part of Inuit life.

After the war the north continued to occupy an important place in the public eye; it was now seen as holding vast mineral resources, which could ensure the future well-being of Canada for centuries to come. Public focus also meant that the media became interested in the north, and began to report and document all facets of the lives of northern people. Stories appeared in the southern press about the plight of the Inuit. It was alleged that thousands of Inuit people were hungry, and many dying of starvation. Canadian author Farley Mowat travelled in the eastern Arctic in the late 1940s and was appalled by the starvation he found. In his book, *People of the Deer*, he describes the extinction by starvation of the Ihalmiut people, and the government's failure to do anything constructive to prevent it.

The federal government realized it had to act. It was decided to move the Inuit to government-built towns. Here, because they were housed in one place, it would be easy for the government to ensure that they were provided with essential services, but relocation, sometimes over great distances, further destroyed the traditional Inuit way of life. The relocation of the Inuit also served a political purpose: it was important for Canada to show the flag, in order to justify her claim to sovereignty in the north. For example, in the early 60s, Inuit from Port Harrison (today Inukjuak), Quebec, were moved to Resolute Bay and Grise Fjord to ensure a Canadian presence in the Arctic archipelago.

Reasons for the forced relocation policy were clearly set out in a 1972 federal government report entitled "Eskimo Housing As Planned Culture Change". A scattered population is difficult to administer, the report argued, and there is less likelihood of starvation if everyone is in a settlement (and according to a 1972 federal government report less likelihood of criticism by the press). It is easier to establish health stations; it is easier to distribute welfare payments. And, though of course it was not stated in the federal report, people are more likely to be assimilated into the mainstream of Canadian society when they are living in communities. It is also much easier to show the flag — to prove sovereignty — when people are living in communities rather than roaming the land in search of game or living in temporary hunting camps.

The report detailed some of the problems that resulted: "…crash programs were undertaken without a clear concept of the role the government wished to assume and what role the government wished Eskimos to assume. The government has created a need on the part of the Eskimo for many material items and services associated with the new housing, and contributed to the acceptance of many Euro-Canadian values and ideas….They were encouraged to buy their own homes, then encouraged to rent them…They are told they must be educated to perform jobs which are their new and future form of subsistence, but then are largely denied jobs other than those in menial capacities. They are told that they must assume responsibility but are not given adequate opportunity to do so."

The north took on even more importance in Canadian thinking during the ascendancy of John Diefenbaker. He came to power promising, amongst other things, the opening of Canada's last frontier, the north. His "roads to resources" policy was a central campaign theme in the 1958 election. "What better preparation for the hundredth anniversary of Confederation could there be than to spend the last decade of our first century as a nation in concentrating on the development of that sparsely populated but tempting four-fifths of our national territory that makes up the Canadian North?" Diefenbaker asked. He pointed to the large cities that had been developed in the Soviet north, and saw no reason why the same could not happen in Canada. He announced a six-year 100-million-dollar plan to develop roads to mineral resources. Not surprisingly, the project paid scant attention to the needs or wishes of northern residents. It was simply assumed that roads and mines would be good for everyone, including those whose livelihood depended on hunting and fishing. Some two decades later, commissions investigating the building of northern pipelines (the Berger and Lysyk inquiries) were to show that such assumptions were questionable.

It was only in the 1970s that native concerns in Canada's last frontier finally came to the forefront of public attention. This was largely thanks to the work of then-Judge Thomas Berger and also to the Lysyk inquiry (chaired by Ken Lysyk, now a judge of the British Columbia Supreme Court). Both inquiries were charged by the federal government with looking at the economic, social and environmental consequences of building a pipeline through northern Canada and both reported to the federal government in 1977. The Berger inquiry examined the feasibility of a pipeline along the Mackenzie Valley; the Lysyk inquiry examined the implications of the Alaska pipeline being built across the southern Yukon. Both inquiries devoted considerable effort to listening to native concerns in native communities. Berger took his inquiry to thirty-five different communities and listened to the evidence of almost 1000 northerners. Both inquiries came to the same conclusion — there had to be a delay in pipeline construction in order to allow native land claims to be settled and to allow native institutions adequate time to acculturate to the new developments.

The Lysyk inquiry concluded "…we consider that a minimum of four years will be necessary to permit sufficient implementation and to avoid prejudice to a just settlement of the Yukon Indian land claim….The risk is that construction of the pipeline may begin before Indian people can mobilize the financial and other resources provided by the settlement to take advantage of the opportunities that its construction may provide."

Thomas Berger came to the same conclusion.
"...The future of the North ought not to be determined
only by our own southern ideas of frontier development. It should also reflect the ideas of the people who
call it their homeland," he said. "Native people desire
a settlement of native claims before a pipeline is built.
They do not want a settlement — in the tradition of
treaties — that will extinguish their rights to the land.
They want a settlement that will entrench their rights
to the land and that will lay the foundations of native
self-determination under the Constitution of
Canada...In my opinion, a period of ten years will be
required in the Mackenzie Valley and Western Arctic
to settle native claims, and to establish the new institutions and new programs that a settlement will entail.
No pipeline should be built until these things have
been achieved," Berger concluded.

The Berger and Lysyk reports put a halt to the
proposed construction projects. Both heard extensive
representation from native peoples. These inquiries
marked what was probably the first time Indians and
Inuit were given an opportunity to speak on national
issues and actually have an influence on policies
profoundly affecting their lives. In fact, these inquiries
probably were the first step in a change in national
policy on native rights, for as the constitutional discussions of the late seventies and eighties were to show,
the Canadian government is at last beginning to consult
native people on matters that concern them.

4
Treaties: For as Long as the Sun Shines...

"With this organization that's being discussed now, finally we're going to have a vehicle in place where Treaty Indians can have their voice heard…just dealing with the treaties," declared the president of the Indian Association of Alberta in 1984, after the formation of the Prairie Treaty Nations Alliance. Prairie Indians have long regarded their treaties as being an essential part of their Indianness. Harold Cardinal, in his *The Unjust Society*, stated, "To the Indians of Canada, the treaties represent an Indian Magna Carta." But while they see the treaties as their Magna Carta, Indian leaders also firmly believe that governments have not lived up to the commitments made in the treaties. Unfortunately, "white man speaks with forked tongue" is not only a line used in cheap westerns. To many Indians, it is simply a statement of the truth.

Two types of treaties were signed with Indians in Canada: peace and friendship treaties, and land rights treaties. When the European powers first arrived in Canada they often made pacts with the Indians, promising friendship if the Indians agreed not to attack or molest them. France was the beneficiary of many of these treaties but the English certainly entered into them as well. They were often broken after a very short time by hostilities, after which yet another treaty of peace would be signed. A typical example was the

Treaty of 1713, signed in Portsmouth, New Hampshire, between the English and area Indians. The treaty provided:

> WHEREAS for some years last past We [the Indians] have made a breach of our Fidelity and Loyalty to the Crowns of Great Britain and have made open Rebellion against her Majesty's Subjects...That at all times forever, from and after the date of these presents, we will cease and forbear all acts of hostility toward all the subjects of the Crown...That her Majesty's Subjects, the English, shall & may peacefully & quietly enter upon, improve & forever enjoy, all and singular their Rights of Land & former Settlements, Properties, & possessions...Wherefore, we...cast ourselves upon her Majesty's mercy for the pardon of all our past rebellions, hostilities, and Violations of our promises, praying to be received unto her Majesty's Grace & Protection...

Over half a dozen treaties of peace and friendship were signed before 1763 between the British and the Indians. The number signed between the French and the Indians is unknown; they were often informal and many were never put into writing.

While such treaties are historically important in determining Indian rights today, the land deals wherein Indians gave up their land rights in return for various benefits and payments are more important. Indians were the owners of valuable real estate, undeveloped and unserviced, which the government wanted for settlement and development. A deal was struck, the Indians sold their real estate, perhaps not for the best price, and today the documentation witnessing that deal is labelled a "treaty". Close to five hundred such land deals have been signed in Canada since the 1700s.

The terms may be different in each case, but in certain essentials there has been an unvarying formula to the negotiations. In fact, one could write a script that would fit them all equally.

Government treaty negotiators kept detailed notes (often made by a secretary — typically male — at the site of the negotiations) and also made detailed reports to their superiors regarding the treaties they had negotiated. In some instances the reports are close to verbatim records of the discussions that took place. Alexander Morris, who negotiated four of the treaties in western Canada, even published a book (*The Treaties of Canada with the Indians*) recounting the negotiations for the western treaties, along with records of his correspondence, and verbatim reports of the discussions. Indians have often referred to such materials, along with oral recollections passed on from generation to generation, to show that the treaties do not contain all the promises made by the government. Such materials also allow us to create the script for a docudrama dealing with the signing of treaties.

A Typical Treaty Negotiation

The fictional script based on reports of treaty negotiations would read as follows:

Plot:

A decision is taken by the authorities (first English, next colonial and finally, after 1867, Canadian) to buy the land that is needed from the Indians. Someone is appointed — in the early years often a military officer, later a government official — to carry out the negotiations. His instructions are to get the land as quickly and as cheaply as possible. A location is selected for the negotiations. Messengers are sent to Indian chiefs occupying the land wanted for settlement, inviting them and their men to the selected location on a certain date so that land surrenders could be negotiated. These invitations are conveyed orally.

The Indians find themselves in a difficult situation. While the territory is supposedly theirs, they have seen squatters and hunters, perhaps even surveyors on their lands. They realize that settlement is encroaching on their lands and they are afraid that whether they agree to a treaty or not their land will be taken for settlement. The encroachment of white settlement means that their supply of food (game animals) is diminishing. In some cases by the time the Indians come to treaty negotiations they are starving. The lack of food, the uncertain future and the use of alcohol have demoralized the Indians to the point of being willing to sign almost anything. Coupled with this, in coming to these meetings the Indians have little idea of what is on the government's agenda, and no idea of what will be involved in the process.

Sometimes the Indians send a message to the government negotiator that they would like a more convenient place for the meeting. The government negotiator inevitably refuses — to agree would be to leave the Indians with the impression that they have bargaining power.

The government negotiator travels out to the meeting site. He may have a militia unit with him, in full dress uniform (lots of red), or perhaps several North-West Mounted Policemen. Several interpreters (often people of mixed blood) also travel with the negotiator. Sometimes there is a problem because the interpreter does not speak the exact dialect required — perhaps Swampy Cree instead of Plains Cree. The negotiator will probably bring food along to feed the Indians at the meeting site and of course various objects to be given to them as presents.

Setting: A small hill in a meadow one kilometre from a trading post. The negotiator's tent is pitched on the hilltop, and the Indian campsite is 300 metres away. In the early morning on the day set for negotiations, a militia officer goes with the interpreter to the Indian camp summoning the Indians to the hilltop. The Indians tell the interpreter they are not ready to negotiate, one of their chiefs has not arrived. They ask for another day. The negotiator is less than happy to hear this. However, he agrees to delay negotiations until mid-afternoon.

3:00 p.m.: Forty Indian males have gathered on the hilltop. A Union Jack flutters in the wind. A militia platoon stands at attention. A clerk sits at a table, ready to note all of the proceedings. Three officials are making idle conversation. One of them, William Burke, has been appointed to carry out these negotiations; he is accompanied by the assistant deputy superintendent general of Indian affairs and a local official. An Anglican minister also accompanies the party.

Burke shakes hands with all the chiefs then begins his speech. Most of the dialogue produced in this fictional account has actually been taken from reports of various treaty negotiations.

Burke: Children. I salute you on behalf of your Great
    Father. We are sent here by the Queen, by the Great
    Mother. She has sent us here to represent her.

A pause occurs while the interpreter translates this.

Burke: (continuing) The Queen loves her red children;
    she has always been friends with them. She knows it is

hard for them to live. We have come here with a message from the Queen and want to tell you all her mind. We want to speak to you about the land and what the Queen is willing to do for you. But before we tell you, we want you to tell us who your Chiefs and headmen are who will speak for you.

The chiefs, speaking through the interpreter, identify themselves.

Burke: We are happy that you are here, my children. The Queen is very concerned about her children whom she loves very much. She wants to tell her children that she wants to help them to help themselves. She wants you to have a place to live where you can grow crops and raise cattle. The country is wide and you are scattered, other people will come in. Now unless the places where you would like to live are secured soon, there might be difficulty. The White Man might come and settle on the very place you would like to be. Now what we would like to do is this: we wish to give you a place where you may live….And we want to help you to learn the cunning of the white man, we want to show you how to grow crops and raise cattle, so that you will never be hungry again.

Buckquaquet: (Chief of the Chippewa) I am glad the Queen wants to talk to us for there are many things which bother us. I am to be pitied, I have no old men to instruct me. I am the head chief, but a young man. Last year so many of our old people were taken away by the Great Spirit. [By a smallpox epidemic].

The translator translates this into English. Proceedings are slow.

Burke: I condole with you for the loss you have met with. It is the will of the Great Spirit to remove our nearest and dearest connections; we must submit to his will and not repine. But the Queen has sent me to speak of the future, so tell me your concerns.

Buckquaquet: Many strangers are coming on our land. They are cutting the trees and the animals are running away. When there are no animals we are hungry. We want to ask the Queen to stop these strangers...

Pahtosh: (another chief) And tell the Queen there is also a log house which the trading company has built and many strangers come to the house bringing furs and taking away many other things in return. All these people coming and going is scaring the game away...

Cahgagewin: (another chief) And last year there were these strange men who came to measure the land...

Burke: That is why the Queen has asked me to come and talk to you. She is very anxious to protect her children. But the Queen has other children besides you and she wants to treat all her children equally. Now who made the earth, the grass, the stone and the wood? The Great Spirit. He made them for all his children to use and now the Queen wants to make sure that the Great Spirit's gift is shared equally by all her children. That is why the Queen wants to give you a place to live which will be your place, a place where the strangers will never be able to bother you; this place will be your reserve.... And the Queen wants to give you money to help you live on this place...every year she will give your Chiefs twenty-five dollars and for each of your headmen she will give ten dollars...and she will also pay each member of the tribe...I know that there are some red men as well as white men who think only of today and never think of tomorrow. The Queen has to think of what will come long after today. Therefore, the promises we have to make to you are not for today only but for tomorrow, not only for you but for your children born and unborn and the promises we make will be carried out as long as the sun shines above and the water flows in the ocean.

Pahtosh: You speak of a place where the strangers will
not bother us — our reserve. All of us — those behind
us — wish to have their reserves marked out, which they
will point out, when the time comes. There is not one
tribe here that has not laid it out.

Burke: As soon as it is convenient to the Government
to send surveyors to lay out the reserves they will do so,
and they will try to suit every particular band.

Buckquaquet: Father, we have heard your words...but
Father, our women and children are very hungry...from
our lands we receive scarcely anything and if your words
are true we will have even less land and less hunting...we
hope that we shall not be prevented from the right of
fishing, and use of the waters, and hunting where we can
find game.

Burke: You want to be at liberty to hunt as before. We
do not want to take that means of living from you. You
have it the same as before, only this, that if a man,
whether Indian, half-breed or white, has a good field of
grain you will not destroy it with your hunt. I have authority to make reserves on which you can hunt and it may
be a long time before the other lands are wanted and in
the meantime you will be permitted to hunt and fish over
them. And the rivers are open to all and you have an
equal right to fish and hunt on them.

Buckquaquet: Father, we have heard your words and
will go to our camp and consult and give you an answer
to the request of our Great Mother, the Queen.

Pahtosh: We have heard all that you have told us, but
I want to tell you how it is with us; when a thing is
thought of quietly, probably that is the best way. I ask
this much from you this day: that we go and think of
your words.

Burke: Yes, that is good, my children. Go to your camp
and consult and when you have made up your minds
come and let me hear what it is.

The next day the Indians send a messenger to say that they are still undecided and need another day. The day after is a Sunday, and the service is celebrated by the Anglican minister who is accompanying the treaty negotiator. The Indians send a message that they are still not ready to continue negotiations, but that they will come to a church service if another is held in the afternoon. A second service is held by Father Merryman for the Indian people.

By 11:00 a.m. on Monday, Commissioner Burke is annoyed that he hasn't heard from the Indians. He sends a messenger to summon the Indians to the hilltop. At 2:00 that afternoon the Indians have assembled.

Burke: Indian children of the Queen, it is four days since I came here. I still have to go further after I leave here and then a long journey home. I have not hurried you, you have had two days to think, I have spoken much to you and now I wish to hear you, my ears are open and I wish to hear the voices of your principal Chiefs or of those chosen to speak for them. Now I am waiting.

Cahgagewin: We have heard your words that you have come to say to us as the representative of the Queen. We were glad to hear what you had to say and have gathered together in council and thought the words over amongst us, we were glad to hear you tell us how we might live by our own work. When I commence to settle on the lands to make a living for myself and my children I beg of you to assist me in every way possible — when I am at a loss how to proceed I want the advice and assistance of the Queen, the children yet unborn I wish you to treat in like manner as they advance in civilization like the white man. This is all I have been told to say now, if I have not said anything in the right manner I wish to be excused; this is the voice of the people.

Burke: I am glad to learn that you Children are looking forward to being civilized. That is the desire of the Queen.

The Queen will send a man to look after the Indians, to be Chief Superintendent of Indian Affairs and under him will be two or three other men to assist him. And when you go to a reserve the Queen will give you a school and a schoolmaster — the Queen would like you to learn something of the cunning of the white man.

Pahtosh: Father, our women and children are very hungry and desired me to ask you to let them taste a little of our Father's provisions and milk...We want to think of our children...it is there we want your aid, when we cannot help ourselves and in case of troubles seen and unforeseen in the future.

Burke: I have told you that the money I have offered you would be paid to you and your children. And to each family that cultivates the soil the Queen will give one spade, two hoes, and one axe, and one plough for every ten families. And we will give you a bull and four cows and some oats and potatoes for seed....And I know that the sympathy of the Queen, and her assistance would be given to you in any unforeseen circumstances. You must trust to the generosity of the Queen. Now I know, from past experience of treaties, that no sooner will we leave than some of you will say this thing and that were promised and the promise was not fulfilled and that you cannot rely on the Queen's representative, that he did not tell the truth, while amongst yourselves are the falsifiers. Now before we rise from here all that you are promised must be understood and it must be in writing; and I hope you will not leave until you thoroughly understand the meaning of every word that comes from us...My words will pass away and so will yours, so our clerk always writes down what I promise, that our children may know what we said and did and our clerk will give you a copy today. And next year I shall send copies of what is written in the treaty printed on skin, so that it cannot rub out nor be destroyed, and one shall be given to each chief so that there may be no mistakes...We have not come here to deceive you, we have not come here to rob you, we have not come here to take away anything that belongs to you...

The Indians ask for a short adjournment in which to consult. After returning, they announce that they are ready to agree. A copy of the treaty is prepared by the clerk and duly signed. Medals bearing the Queen's likeness are presented to the chiefs along with suits of clothing. After these gifts to the chiefs, presents are distributed to the rest of the Indians including pork, flour, blankets, twine, powder, ammunition and some hand tools.

A Typical Treaty

The above script is a condensed version of the type of discussions that took place. Treaty negotiations sometimes went on for days. Generally, the same points were covered in treaty negotiations, and many treaties, especially the numbered treaties of the late 1800s, contain many similar terms. The numbered treaties dealt with reserves, annual payments, agriculture, schools and other issues. Treaty Six (covering central Saskatchewan and Alberta) is instructive. It provides for:

- a surrender of Indian rights and title to the lands covered by the treaty and covering 121,000 square miles;
- the creation of reserves not to exceed one square mile per family of five;
- the location of the reserves to be determined, after consultation with the Indians, by someone sent by the chief superintendent of Indian affairs;

- each man, woman and child to receive twelve dollars on the signing of the treaties;
- the government to maintain schools on the reserve;
- a ban on intoxicating liquors on reserves;
- a guarantee of hunting and fishing rights;
- the government having the right to take reserve land with compensation, for public works;
- a census of all Indians to be undertaken by the government;
- an annual payment of five dollars per person;
- $1,500 per year to be spent by the government for twine and ammunition;
- if reserve residents wish to farm they are to receive four hoes, two spades, two hay forks, two reaping hooks, two axes, two scythes, and one whetstone per family; one plough and one harrow for every three families; one cross-saw, one hand-saw, one pit-saw, necessary files, one grindstone, one auger for each band and also enough wheat, oats, barley and potatoes for seed; each band also to get four oxen, one bull, six cows, one boar and two sows, and one handmill; finally each chief was to get a chest of carpenter's tools (these were one-time gifts and were designed to encourage Indians to become farmers);
- each chief to receive an annual salary of twenty-five dollars, each headman fifteen dollars and a suit of clothes every three years for both chiefs and headmen. Upon signing, each chief was also to receive a medal, a flag, one horse, harness and a wagon;
- the government to help in event of famine or pestilence (this clause was unique to Treaty Six);
- an annual grant of $1000 (for the first three years) to assist with agriculture;

- a medicine chest to be kept on the reserve (this clause did not appear in any other treaty, and the courts have split on whether this clause means free medical care);
- the signing Indians agreeing to obey the treaty and to conduct themselves as good and loyal subjects;
- the signing Indians agreeing to be law-abiding and to maintain peace and order.

The Métis and Treaties

In writing his book, *The Treaties of Canada with the Indians*, Morris raised the question of the Métis and put them into three categories; the farmer, "the second class who have been recognized as Indians, and have passed into the bands among whom they reside," and those who live by the buffalo hunt.

Thus, it is not surprising that in some instances treaties cover Métis. The Lake Huron and Lake Superior Treaties of 1850 (often referred to as the Robinson Treaties) included 284 Métis and 2,662 Indians. In negotiating Treaty Three, Alexander Morris reported: "They (the Indians) said there were some ten to twenty families of half-breeds who were recognized as Indians, and lived with them, and they wished them included. I said the treaty was not for whites, but I would recommend that those families should be permitted the option of taking either status as Indians or whites, but that they could not take both." The Métis of Rainy River signed an agreement in 1875 wherein they agreed to abide by and be part of Treaty Three. A reserve of eighteen square miles was set aside for them to live in.

The practice of giving Métis living with Indians the option of taking treaty continued in later treaty negotiations. Sometimes they were asked to choose between being part of the treaty agreement or accepting scrip, a piece of paper entitling them to a parcel of land or money. Some Métis who agreed to abide by treaty later changed their minds and took scrip.

Some Questions About Treaties

In our fictional script, no mention was made of the land belonging to the Indians or the government wanting to buy it. This was the case in most treaty negotiations. It is often assumed that treaty negotiations dealt specifically with the land ownership issue. They did not, yet the actual treaty documents are written in language that makes it quite clear that Indians are giving up their land rights. Typical of the legalese found in treaties is the language found in Treaty Eight, signed in 1899 and covering northern Alberta and small portions of Saskatchewan, British Columbia and the Northwest Territories

> ...the said Indians DO HEREBY CEDE, RELEASE, SURRENDER AND YIELD UP [the capitalization in original] to the Government of the Dominion of Canada, for Her Majesty the Queen and Her successors for ever all their rights, titles and privileges whatsoever, to the lands included with the following limits, that is to say: [Here a paragraph was inserted describing the land surrendered]

> AND ALSO the said Indian rights, titles, privileges whatsoever to all other lands wherever situated in the Northwest Territories, British Columbia, or in any other portion of the Dominion of Canada.

> TO HAVE AND TO HOLD the same to her Majesty the Queen and her successors for ever.

Another example is Treaty Twenty, covering territory around Peterborough, Ontario, and signed in 1818. It provided:

> And the said Buckquaquet, Pishikinse, Pahtosh, Cahgahkishinse, Cahgaewin and Pininse, as well for themselves as for the Chippewa Nation inhabiting and claiming the said tract of land as above described, do freely, fully and voluntarily surrender and convey the same to His Majesty without reservation or limitation in perpetuity.

The wording in all the other treaties is similar to the above examples. It is wording copied from English real estate law developed to describe the legal effect when someone transfers his title to another. An interesting question arises, in view of the fact that little discussion about title to land took place during treaty negotiations: did the Indian chiefs who signed these treaties truly appreciate the legal consequences of the documents they signed? They were not familiar with the language and were in most cases dealing through translators. Words like ''surrender'', ''convey'', ''cede'', ''yield up'', ''release'', while having a precise legal meaning, probably meant nothing to the Indian leaders — especially after they were translated. They had no understanding of English legal concepts and their concepts of property were very different from those of the negotiators.

In Canadian law, contracts can be set aside if it can be proved that one of the parties to a contract was of unsound mind, was pressured to sign the contract (called *duress* in law), was being unfairly taken advantage of, or was clearly unaware of the consequences of the contract he was signing. To date, only one Indian group has yet tried to set aside a treaty. While having some success at the trial level, their case was lost at the appeal on other grounds. Of course, if a treaty were successfully challenged, one result would be that the Indians would then have no treaty. They would be in the same position as Indian groups in British Columbia and the north who are currently trying to negotiate land claim settlements.

The fact that the two parties were not equals at the negotiating table has prompted legal scholars to ask whether treaties should be interpreted strictly. A 1983 Supreme Court of Canada decision declared that "...treaties and statutes relating to Indians should be liberally construed and doubtful expressions resolved in favour of the Indian.... Indian treaties must be construed, not according to the technical meaning of their words, but in a sense in which they would naturally be understood by the Indians."

The problem also arises that sometimes promises made during negotiations did not appear in the treaty. The question arises whether the Crown is bound by such promises. And in other instances, oral promises made during negotiations appear in a form different from that negotiated by the parties. Treaty Eight, discussed above, is an example in point. During its negotiation in 1899, Commissioner David Laird reported, "there was expressed at every point the fear...that the treaty would lead to taxation....We assured them that the treaty...did not open the way to the imposition of any tax..." The treaty, however, is silent about taxation. What then is the legal effect of Laird's promise?

Similarly, on Indian concerns about the right to hunt for food, Laird reported that "...we had to solemnly assure them that only such laws as to hunting and fishing as were in the interest of the Indians and were found necessary in order to protect the fish and fur-bearing animals would be made, and that they would be as free to hunt and fish after the treaty as they would be if they never entered into it.''

Treaty Eight contains a guarantee of hunting and fishing rights. However, since those guarantees were made this right has been limited by the Natural Resources Transfer Agreement and by such federal legislation as the Migratory Birds Convention Act.

The courts have had to deal with the issue of prom-ises made that never appeared in the text of the treaty. On June 11, 1977, two Indians by the names of Taylor and Williams were caught taking sixty-five bullfrogs from Crowe Lake in Peterborough County. They were charged with violating Ontario's Game and Fish Act by taking bullfrogs during closed season. The bullfrogs were taken from unoccupied Crown lands, for food. These Indians were covered by the Treaty of 1818, which was silent as to the right to hunt. However, the accused argued that their right to take game was assured orally — this was confirmed by written reports made at the time of the treaty negotiations. The Ontario Court of Appeal held that the oral assurances should be considered in interpreting treaties. As a result, the court ruled that treaty included the right to hunt and fish. The Indians were acquitted. Under the Indian Act (a federal law) an Indian treaty takes priority over provincial law.

While the courts have (at least in recent years) taken the view that treaties should be liberally interpreted they have also held that treaties with Indians are not international treaties — that is, between nations. Not only are they not international agreements, some judges have gone so far as to suggest that treaties with Indians are nothing more than mere promises by the Crown. Of course, one need not be a lawyer to know what a promise is worth.

Two Categories of Treaties

Treaties signed in Canada dealing with Indian land rights can be divided into two categories, those signed before 1850, and those signed after. Most pre-1850 treaties involved fairly small parcels of land. For example, in 1764 (a year after the Royal Proclamation of 1763) Sir William Johnson, superintendent general of Indian affairs, purchased a two-mile strip of land on the left bank of the Niagara River from the Seneca tribe of the Six Nations Confederacy. By contrast, treaties signed after 1850 tended to cover vast tracts of land. Treaty Three, signed in 1873, covered 55,000 square miles (142,500 square kilometres) in northwestern Ontario. Treaty Six, 1876, covered over 120,000 square miles (310,780 square kilometres) in central Saskatchewan and Alberta. This difference is accounted for by the pattern of settlement. Until the opening up of the west began, settlement progressed at a fairly slow pace; there was no need for great parcels of land, hence land claim settlements were generally small in territorial scope.

There were other major differences between pre- and post-1850 treaties. Many treaties prior to 1850 involved a one-time payment to the Indians for land surrendered. All the treaties after 1850 include annual payments, often referred to as treaty money. Although many people believe that all Indians receive treaty money, the truth is that only those Indians covered by treaties that provide for an annual payment (essentially those on the prairies and in northwestern Ontario) receive treaty payments.

While the system of regular payments to Indians was finally implemented on a wide basis in 1850, the idea had been conceived much earlier. As early as 1752, in the Treaty or Articles of Peace and Friendship Renewed, signed in Halifax by three Micmac chiefs, provision was made for the Indians to receive half-yearly "bread, flour and such other Provisions, as can be procured...". While the idea of an annual payment of goods thus dates back to the 1700s the idea of money payment came to the fore after the War of 1812.

Land was needed for Ontario to grow. This, of course, meant dealing with the Indian situation. The Lords of the Treasury in London (England) declared that the cost of land required for expansion would have to be paid by Upper Canada. Lieutenant-Governor Maitland devised a plan to sell Indian lands at public auction. Purchasers would be required to pay 10 per cent down and carry a mortgage for the balance. However, as long as purchasers paid the annual interest they were not required to make payments on principal. The income from the interest payments would then be used to make annual payments, in perpetuity, to Indians who sold their lands. Thus came about the concept of an annual treaty payment. The offer of an annual payment in perpetuity was often used as an inducement to encourage Indians to enter into a treaty. It probably had some success. In the decade after the War of 1812 2.8 million hectares (6.9 million acres) of Indian land passed to government control.

How much were the annual payments? In 1818 the Chippewa nation, living in what is today the Peterborough area, surrendered 1,951,000 acres (789,500 hectares) for an annual payment of £740 (British). In 1850 government negotiator William Robinson received the surrender of large parcels of land on the north shores of Lakes Superior and Huron from the Ojibewa Indians of Lake Huron for £2000 (Upper Canadian) and an annual payment of £600. (These treaties are often called the Robinson Treaties.) After 1850, the practice was started of paying the annuity to individuals, rather than as a lump sum to the band. Thus Treaty Three (1873) provided for a payment of twelve dollars to each Indian upon signing of the treaty and an annual payment of five dollars in perpetuity. Women and children were included as recipients of payments. The five-dollar payment was included in most of the later numbered treaties (including all women and children) and is still distributed today on Treaty day. In many of the treaties after Two, an annual payment to the chief of twenty-five dollars and fifteen dollars for headmen was included. At the time of signing, five dollars represented a substantial sum of money. It is now insignificant to say the least — and of course, none of the treaties had an inflation factor built in.

Many early Indian treaties did not provide for the setting aside of reserves; after 1850, they all did. In treaties One and Two (both signed in 1871 and covering parts of southern Manitoba) 160 acres was set aside for each family of five. Starting with Treaty Three in 1873 the land allotment for reserves was raised to one square mile for each family of five. While the treaties set aside land for the use of Indians the title or ownership in this land remained, and still remains, with the Crown. Thus while Indians can use reserves the legal title remains with the federal government. The Robinson Treaties reserved specified parcels of land as reserves. Treaties One, Two, Five and Seven provided for the establishment of reserves near specified rivers and lakes. The balance of the numbered treaties (Three, Four, Six, Eight and Ten) provided that the location of reserves was to be determined by later consultation. In many cases the process of setting aside the required lands for reserves has still not been completed.

Treaty Hunting Rights

A common feature of most treaties, both pre- and post-1850, was the guarantee of hunting and fishing rights. Even some of the Treaties of Friendship and Peace assured Indians the right to hunt and fish. "Saving unto the said Indians their own Grounds, & free liberty for Hunting, Fishing, Fowling...," declared the Treaty of 1713.

The hunting rights guaranteed by the Treaty of 1752 were at issue in the case involving James Simon, a Micmac Indian of the Shubenacadie Indian Brook band in Nova Scotia. He was charged with possessing ammunition and a rifle in deer country contrary to the Nova Scotia Lands and Forests Act. Simon argued that he was a descendant of the Indians who had signed the treaty of 1752, which guaranteed "free liberty to hunt and fish as usual". The Crown questioned whether the treaty was valid, whether it had not been invalidated by subsequent hostilities and whether the accused was in fact a beneficiary of the treaty. The Supreme Court of Canada ruled that the treaty was valid and held that the guarantee of hunting rights overrode provincial legislation (by section 88 of the Indian Act, provincial laws only apply to Indians if they do not conflict with any treaties or federal law).

In later treaties a hunting guarantee, which appeared in almost every treaty, provided:

> And Her Majesty the Queen HEREBY AGREES with the said Indians that they shall have right to pursue

their usual vocations of hunting, trapping and fishing throughout the tract surrendered as heretobefore described, subject to such regulations as may from time to time be made by the Government of the country, acting under the authority of Her Majesty, and saving and excepting such tracts as may be required or taken up from time to time for settlement, mining, lumbering, trading or other purposes.

Indians have regarded these guarantees as providing them the unfettered right to hunt and fish. Governments have not always agreed. The federal government has passed the Migratory Birds Convention Act dealing with the hunting of migratory birds such as ducks and geese. The courts have held that the act applies to Indians and overrides the promises made in the treaties. The federal Fisheries Act similarly overrides treaty fishing rights. These acts are often cited by Indians as examples of how treaty promises have been broken.

On May 7, 1962, Michael Sikyea shot a mallard duck on a pond near the Yellowknife airport. He was an Indian covered by Treaty Eleven, which contained a hunting clause similar to the one reproduced above. He was charged with contravening the Migratory Birds Convention Act by hunting out of season. Sikyea supported himself and his family by hunting. He argued that his treaty gave him the right to hunt in spite of what the act said. His case went to the Supreme Court of Canada but at both the Supreme Court of Canada and the Court of Appeal level, the courts ruled that he was subject to the Migratory Birds Convention Act. In his judgement at the Court of Appeal level, Mr. Justice Johnson commented on the conflict between the treaty and the act:

It is, I think, clear that the rights given to the Indians by their treaties as they apply to migratory birds have been taken away by this Act and its Regulations. How are we to explain this apparent breach of faith on the part of the Government, for I cannot think it can be described in any other terms? This cannot be described as a minor or insignificant curtailment of these treaty rights, for game birds have always been a most plentiful, a most reliable and a readily obtainable food in large areas of Canada. I cannot believe that the Government of Canada realized that in implementing the Convention they were at the same time breaching the treaties that they had made with the Indians. It is much more likely that these obligations under the treaties were overlooked — a case of the left hand having forgotten what the right hand had done. The subsequent history of the Government's dealing with the Indians would seem to bear this out.

Perhaps the judge was being overly generous in characterizing this as a case of the left hand not knowing what the right was doing. In 1911, Frank Oliver, minister of the interior and in charge of Indian affairs, stated:

For while we believe that the Indian having a certain treaty right is entitled ordinarily to stand upon that right and get benefit of it, yet we believe that there are circumstances and conditions in which the Indian by standing on his treaty rights does himself an ultimate injury, as well as does an injury to the white people, whose interests are brought into immediate conjunction with the interests of the Indians.

In view of such statements its not surprising the government has occasionally overridden treaty rights.

Since 1982 treaty rights have been enshrined in the Constitution, which states, ''The existing aboriginal and treaty rights of the aboriginal peoples of Canada

are hereby recognized and affirmed.'' According to
court decisions to date that provision does not restore
treaty rights that have been taken away. However, it
should provide protection against further encroachment.

Current Issues

Today there are a number of major complaints regarding treaties, in particular the prairie treaties. First, not
all the land that was supposed to be set aside for Indian
reserves ever was. Second, some of the land that was
set aside for Indian reserves was then taken for settlement, in dubious circumstances.

In Saskatchewan alone the Indian estimate is that
an additional 2.9 million acres of land has to be set
aside to satisfy the terms of the treaties. In 1976 the
federal government, the Saskatchewan government and
the Federation of Saskatchewan Indians agreed in principle that outstanding treaty land entitlements should
be settled in Saskatchewan. The formula agreed upon
was 128 acres muliplied by the 1976 Indian population.
(Under most western treaties, reserves of 640 acres
per family of five were granted — this works out to
128 acres per person). By comparison, one million
acres is the approximate size of Saskatchewan's Prince
Albert National Park. Since the conclusion of this
agreement, progress on fulfilling the promised land
entitlement has gone at a snail's pace, though a few
agreements have been concluded.

Some Indians in treaty areas may not be covered by
treaties. They may have been out on the hunt when
the treaties were signed and the census of Indians taken.
Perhaps their band was never notified of the negotiations, and thus never participated. Perhaps they were

notified but refused to participate. Or perhaps the band moved into the treaty area after the treaty was signed. Whatever the reason, there are Indian groups, in treaty areas, who are pressing the federal government to negotiate claims settlements with them because they allege they were never covered by the treaties when they were negotiated. To date the federal government has been reluctant to move quickly on any such claims.

Another issue deals with treaties and self-government. The treaties are silent as to whether Indians still have the right to govern their own affairs. Clearly they had such a right before the arrival of the Europeans. And in most cases they ran their own affairs until the signing of the treaties. Some Indian leaders argue that, as they did not give up their right to self-government in the treaties, it still continues.

It was to deal with such unanswered questions that the federal government in 1985 initiated the treaty renovation process. Treaty Eight was the first to be examined. At the 1985 constitutional conference on aboriginal rights, Prime Minister Mulroney stated that he hoped the Treaty Eight renovation would produce a model that would "provide us with a guide for building a positive, constructive relationship with other aboriginal communities."

Frank Oberle, a Conservative cabinet minister and a longtime member of Parliament, was chosen to serve as a special envoy in the Treaty Eight renovation process. He looked at such issues as unfulfilled land entitlements, hunting and fishing rights and social conditions.

In his report, made public in May 1986, Oberle recommended appointment of a treaty commissioner with the status of a federal minister of state to carry out the treaty renovation negotiations. Part of the commissioner's role will be to spend the first part of his/her mandate in communicating and discussing the renewal process with all people concerned. He recommends that mutually acceptable guidelines be drawn up for the renovation process. He suggests that the Indian Act be suspended in Treaty Eight in favour of a renovated treaty, which would deal with self-government and land issues. Such a renovated agreement would be constitutionally entrenched.

Oberle's report has received considerable favourable support from Indian leaders. However, there are those who argue that they don't need renovated treaties, only a commitment by governments to honor treaties' terms as they already exist.

5
The Indian Act and Indian Affairs Bureaucracy

Life in a dictatorship means many restrictions and few freedoms. Citizens are subject to the whims and caprices of uncaring officials (sometimes having police powers). These officials not only have control over people's lives but also act as prosecutors and judges when citizens break a rule. It goes without saying, of course, that there is no right to vote. There are restrictions on travel; travel passes are required. Career choices are dictated. Children may be taken to state-run residential schools, to ensure that they are indoctrinated with the right values; in fact, there may be a law stating that parents have no authority over their children while they are at the state-run residential school. There are restrictions on property and civil rights. Members of minorities are restricted in using their language and practising their culture. Citizens show little initiative because it is rarely rewarded and often punished. They may even be described as lazy and good for nothing. But the state will certainly not be unhappy with their docility; after all, docile citizens are not causing any trouble.

While that might be an accurate description of life under a dictatorship it also accurately describes the conditions of life that Canada's Indian people lived under for many years and to some extent are still subject to. Canada's national policy was to ''civilize'' the

Indian and, until he was civilized, to protect him from the evils of society. To achieve these aims policy-makers decided they would have to regulate the lives of Canada's native people. It was only in the late 1950s and early 1960s that the burden of regulation began to be lifted from the Indian's shoulders.

Reserves were created for Indians to live on and officials were appointed (usually known as Indian agents) to control activities on the reserve and to enforce federal Indian legislation. The powers of the agents were so extensive that for a number of decades prairie Indians were not even allowed to leave their reserve without a pass from an agent. Of course, many agents were generous, but they had dictatorial powers over reserve life. Some of the rules that Indian agents enforced were found in the Indian Act, first passed by the federal Parliament in 1876; others originated in bureaucratic practice or government policy. Some of the rules and regulations were simply a matter of local officials, far from Ottawa, acting as they saw fit.

"Here I was a young kid in his early twenties and I was absolutely astounded at the power I had over the life of these people...I was really wet behind the ears and here I was telling all these people two and three times older how they should live," a high official with Indian Affairs said recently, describing the start of his career as an Indian agent.

The extent of the powers Indian agents had can be judged from this story, told by a Saskatchewan lawyer, recounting how he became interested in Indian issues in the 1930s. "I was contacted by some Indians to defend a friend of theirs who had been charged with theft, which had supposedly occurred on the reserve. I contacted the Indian agent who I was told was prosecuting the case. Well, he told me to forget it because the guy was guilty. I asked him how he could be so sure and he told me he was going to be the judge as well. I tell you that made me mad.''

Implementing National Policy

Canada's Indian policy was twofold, and underlying all of these restrictions was an attempt by the federal government to implement its Indian policy. That policy included the purchase of those Indian lands needed for settlement, and a drive to civilize and assimilate the Indian. To achieve the latter, policy-makers felt the Indian had to be kept separate from the mainstream of Canadian society.

To implement the first part of its policy the government entered into treaties with Indians. That worked satisfactorily in those areas, like the prairies, where Ottawa had full control over the land. It didn't work in other areas, such as British Columbia, where the colonial government didn't agree with Ottawa's policies.

To implement the civilization aspect of its policy, Ottawa passed the Indian Act: it was a catalogue of restrictions, which Ottawa made use of as a tool for setting out the rules regarding the governing of reserves. A bureaucracy flourished in order to implement the land acquisitions policy and also to enforce the Indian Act. Sometimes the bureaucracy acted overzealously, enforcing non-existent regulations. Sometimes there was confusion in the bureaucracy, because federal policy was not always clear cut. Sometimes the bureaucracy operated with little understanding of Indian people; decisions were made in Ottawa by people far removed from Indian communities. Sometimes the Indian Affairs bureacracy clashed with other departments, and sometimes there was conflict between the federal and provincial bureaucracies. The net result was that the machinery for implementing Indian policy often operated in chaos.

Of course, creating the Indian Affairs bureaucracy was no easy matter. There were decades of confusion over which government department should be responsible for Indian affairs. Until the 1830s Indian matters were largely left to the military. The Indians were required as allies (first in the fight against the French and then in the fight against the Americans), and later were deemed to be a possible threat to settlement.

In 1830, Indian matters in Upper Canada were turned over to the lieutenant governor of the colony, and the reserve system was instituted as a way of training Indians to become farmers. In Lower Canada (Quebec), Indian matters remained in military hands until Lower and Upper Canada were joined as the Province of Canada in 1840, at which time all Indian matters were transferred to the governor general. However, while the governor general was given this responsibility, the Act of Union made no provision for the establishment of an Indian Department and included no budget for Indian matters. It was not until 1860 that full control of Indian matters was given to the colonies. With the transfer of control came a greater involvement by government in Indian life. As long as Indian matters remained the responsibility of the British military, and later of the British Colonial Office, Indians retained a fair degree of self-government. The Colonial Office was far away and cared little about colonial matters.

Confederation in 1867 did not clarify things. The British North America Act made ''Indians and lands reserved for Indians'' a matter of federal responsibility. Until 1873 Indian affairs were left to the secretary of state, after which they were transferred to the newly created Department of the Interior, which was charged with the major task of opening up the west. Naturally, Indian matters played a minor role in the department's overall operations. In 1880, a separate Indian Department was set up; it reported, however, to the minister of the interior, John A. Macdonald, who was also prime minister. His only interest in Indian policy was to ensure that Indians didn't prevent the implementation of his "national dream".

In 1936 the department was made a branch of the Department of Mines and Resources; in 1949 it was transferred to the Department of Citizenship and Immigration. Sixteen years later it was transferred to the Department of Northern Affairs and National Resources. Finally, in 1966, a Department of Indian Affairs and Northern Development was established, with a cabinet minister responsible for the department. With no minister solely responsible for Indian affairs for many years and with the bureaucratic shifts over the years, it is not surprising that Indian policy and its implementation remained in a slough of uncertainty for decades.

Of course, native affairs is big government business and Indian Affairs is not the only department that concerns itself with native matters. Some fourteen federal government departments, ranging from Health and Welfare to the Office of the Secretary of State, have native programs. This does not include the various provincial agencies that run native programs. Some provinces even have native affairs secretariats, which are like mini-Indian Affairs Departments.

The Indian Act

While many government departments (both federal and

provincial) are involved in the native programming, the primary responsibility for Indian programs still rests with the Department of Indian Affairs, whose main tool is the Indian Act, first passed by Parliament in 1876. The Indian Act was not, however, the first federal legislation dealing with Indians. After Confederation the new Dominion quickly started passing laws dealing with Indians, first in 1868, then in 1869. The philosophy and purpose of Indian legislation passed by Parliament in the late 1860s was set out by the deputy superintendent of the Indian Branch in his 1871 report:

> The Acts framed in the years 1868 and 1869, relating to Indian Affairs, were designed to lead the Indian people by degrees to mingle with the white race in the ordinary avocations of life.

When Parliament passed the 1876 Indian Act, it was not a new piece of legislation, but a consolidation of various existing federal and colonial statutes. The essential thrust of the Indian Act was to make Indians wards of the state. While the Indian Act over the years has allowed the existence of band governments (called band councils), the power of such councils has generally been restricted to such unimportant things as controlling dogs on the reserve. Even then, this power was subject to the overriding authority of the Department of Indian Affairs. The self-government talks now under way are looking at ways to increase the powers of band councils.

Restrictions of the Indian Act

It was in personal liberties that the restrictions of the Indian Act were most felt; a whole series of restrictions were introduced between 1880 and 1930 in an attempt to destroy Indianness. Thus, the 1876 Act provided that an Indian could not be a lawyer, doctor, or minister, or hold a university degree, and remain an Indian. In short, one had to choose between being Indian and getting an education. The hope was that Indians would choose education.

Early Indian Acts were aimed at eradicating Indian culture with the hope the Indian would be assimilated. Indian Act legislation outlawed various Indian dances and festivals (such as the potlatch and the sundance) and made it an offence for western Canadian Indians to appear in aboriginal costume off the reserve without permission of the Indian agent. The potlatch ceremony of the west coast Indians, which often involved the giving away of one's property, was of particular concern to federal bureaucrats and legislators. It was described by local Indian agents and missionaries as ''debauchery of the worst kind'' and was considered by the deputy superintendent of Indian affairs as having ''pernicious effects'' on Indians. The potlatch was first outlawed in 1884 at a time when the federal government was trying to inculcate the idea of private ownership in Indians. Five years later, in 1889, the commissioner of Indian affairs reported that:

> The policy of destroying the tribal or communist system is assailed in every possible way and every effort made to implant a spirit of individual responsibility instead.

Prairie Indians were prohibited from selling produce raised or harvested on the reserve unless they had permission from the Indian agent. That prohibition was still on the books in 1986, though bands could be exempted from its application. Similarly, Indians could be prohibited from going to a poolroom for up to a year if the Indian agent or other court official felt that the Indian was inordinately frequenting a poolroom. Along the same lines in 1886 it became an offence for an Indian to gamble; contravention meant a fine of a least ten dollars, with half of the fine going to an informer if there was one. Of course it goes without saying that Indians could not legally consume or possess alcohol either on or off the reserve. Not only was it an offence for an Indian to possess alcohol but if an Indian refused to say where and from whom he got the alcohol, he could be convicted of a further offence. Ironically, the restriction on use of liquor on reserves was one of the few that received support from the Indians. In fact, at the request of the Indians, the federal government in Treaties One to Six specifically promised to exclude liquor from reserves. Even today many Indian communities have voted to remain dry, though these provisions have sometimes been seen by the courts as violating the Bill of Rights and the Charter of Rights and Freedoms.

There were other restrictions, however, which did not receive the support of Indian communities. At one period Indian children were removed from their families and taken to residential schools in order to be removed from the influences of home life. The law prescribed that parents had no authority over their children when they were in residential school.

Other restrictions included limitations on the right of an Indian living on a reserve to make a will. An Indian's will could only be valid if approved by the Indian Affairs Department. This law remains in force.

The issuance of food rations was yet another way in which Indian lives were controlled. At various times in the late 1800s and early 1900s, the depletion of game meant that Indians found themselves dependent upon the good will of the federal government for survival. A system of issuing food rations was developed in the late 1800s and continued until well into the twentieth century. The threat of withdrawal of rations was often used to keep Indians in line. And it was not unknown for so-called good Indians (of which the Indian agent was the sole judge) to get extra rations. The Indians of the prairies, in particular, were starving in the 1880s (after the disappearance of the buffalo) and the ration system coupled with the pass system was used as a way of controlling them and keeping them passive during the 1885 Rebellion. After agents stopped physically distributing food ("I can still remember the agent slicing of a chunk of bacon for us", an Indian elder reminisced recently), food vouchers were issued, which were cashable at local stores. These vouchers did not allow Indians the luxury of choice; the vouchers listed exactly what Indians could buy in the way of food. This was a good example of the contradictions that were often found in Canada's Indian policy. While supposedly Indians were to be integrated into the mainstream of Canadian society, it is difficult to see how this was to be achieved if Indians were not even to be allowed to decide what groceries to buy.

The Pass System

Perhaps the most insidious form of control over the lives of Indians was the "pass system", wherein prairie Indians were not permitted to leave the reserve without a pass. Even if a person wanted to visit a relative on another reserve, pick berries outside the reserve boundary, or go to town for supplies, he needed a pass.

The idea of a pass was first suggested by the deputy superintendent of Indian affairs in the early 1880s but it was not until 1885 that it was instituted. On May 6, 1885, Major General Frederick Middleton, on his way to Batoche to fight the Métis, suggested to Indian Commissioner Edgar Dewdney that a proclamation be issued requiring Indians to remain on their reserve unless they had permission to leave. Middleton wanted to keep the Indians out of the North-West Rebellion. Dewdney replied that he had issued a "notice advising Indians to stay on Reserves and warning them of risks they run in being found off them but have no power to issue proclamation as you suggest." In spite of Dewdney's concern for the legalities of such restrictions, Hayter Reed, the assistant Indian commissioner for the Northwest Territories, Manitoba and Keewatin, informed Dewdney in August 1885 that "I am adopting the system of keeping the Indians on their respective Reserves and not allowing any to leave them without passes..."

By 1886 the system was formalized. Books of passes were issued to Indian agents. The police were instructed to pick up any Indian who could not produce a pass. To get a pass one had to produce a letter of recommendation from his farm instructor. To enforce the pass system the government not only used the police but also threatened to cut off the rations of any Indian who left the reserve without a pass. In view of the scarcity of game on the prairies in the 1880s and '90s the threat of cutting off rations certainly carried considerable clout.

The rationale for the pass system was complex. First, it originated out of a genuine fear that there would be a massive Indian uprising in 1885. Indians who had acted in an "unsatisfactory" manner during the rebellion had this noted on any pass they were issued after 1885. After the North-West Rebellion ended, the system was maintained as a way of forcing Indians to remain on the reserve. John A. Macdonald was trying to get the west settled as part of his national policy and he wanted to make sure settlers were not scared off by roaming Indians. Reserves were created as a civilizing mechanism and in particular as a way of teaching the Indians to farm. Hence the requirement in the early days for a letter of recommendation from the farming instructor; it ensured that the Indian had done all his farm work before he left the reserve. The system was also justified on the basis that Indians should be kept away from the evils of urban life (alcohol, prostitution, gambling) until they were civilized.

Legally, neither the Indian Act nor any other federal legislation allowed the Department of Indian Affairs to institute such a system. The North-West Mounted Police recognized its illegality; in 1891, Commissioner S.B. Steele of the NWMP reported that his men were doing their best to turn back Indians without passes in the Fort Macleod district but that "…a difficulty arises in the fact that few of our men can speak sufficient Blackfoot to make themselves understood and the Indians when it suits their purpose can be very obtuse: they are aware too that we have no legal right to turn them back." A year later government lawyers advised that the system was illegal. When the NWMP temporarily stopped enforcing the pass system in 1893 there was a howl of public protest. While the police vacillated about enforcing the system, it was through the issuance of rations that Indian Affairs made the system work. Simply put, Indians were hungry and to be fed they had to play along with the rules.

The pass system continued until the 1930s. It is generally believed the system was restricted to the area covered by treaties Four, Six, and Seven (generally Saskatchewan and Alberta). Because the system was illegal, records on it are scant and therefore the extent to which it was used remains uncertain.

Residential Schools

Another sad chapter in the implementation of Canadian Indian policy was the residential and industrial school system. All of the treaties in western Canada specifically promised education. It was something that the Indians had asked for at the time of treaty negotiation. Typically, the treaties promised that schools would be built and teachers would be paid. In eastern Canada the education of Indian children was left to various religious orders, who established residential schools with the support of government grants.

In considering how to fulfil its treaty obligations in western Canada the federal government considered three options: they included day schools on the reserve, boarding schools near the reserve, and residential schools far removed from the reserve. In the United States the government had established denominational industrial boarding schools. This was the model adopted in Canada; in the 1880s, to satisfy treaty obligations, the federal government established three industrial schools: Fort Qu'appelle and Battleford in Saskatchewan, and High River in Alberta. However, except for this token effort, the federal government was quite content to make grants to the churches, handing over responsibility for Indian education to them. The churches, in turn, carried out this responsibility by establishing residential schools.

Indians had to be civilized and to accomplish this the authorities felt the children had to be removed from the home environment. As Clifford Sifton, Canada's minister of the interior, stated in condemning the establishment day schools on reserves, "the Indian children are not removed from the surroundings which tend to keep them in a state of more or less degradation."

It was also accepted by officials at the time that Indians did not have the ability to reach the same level of educational achievement as whites. Again speaking in 1903, Sifton stated:

> I have no hesitation in saying — we may as well be frank — that the Indian cannot go out from school, making his own way and compete with the white man...He has not the physical, mental or moral get-up to enable him to compete. He cannot do it."

It was assumed, therefore, that the most that could be expected of an Indian was for him/her to learn a trade, and consequently the schools took on the character of industrial or training schools.

To call them "schools" may well be a misnomer. Children often ran away; in fact, it became necessary to pass a law stating that Indian parents had no authority over their children in residential schools so that runaways could be returned. The Mounties were even asked to assist with the task and were charged with returning stray children to the residential school. It doesn't take much imagination to think of the trauma a young child must have suffered in being taken away from his or her parents to a strange environment many hundreds of kilometres away. Indian languages were forbidden, as was the practice of any form of Indian culture. After all, the purpose of the schools was to break the Indian of his/her ways. Of course it goes without saying that because many of the schools were denominational, they put considerable effort into Christianizing Indians.

In the early days the schools were destructive not only of culture but even of life itself. Duncan Campbell Scott (a well-known Canadian poet and a former deputy superintendent general of Indian affairs) writing in *Canada and Its Provinces* in 1914 concluded:

> ...the system was open to criticism. Insufficient care was exercised in the admission of children to the schools. The well-known predisposition of Indians to tuberculosis resulted in a very large percentage of deaths among the pupils. They were housed in buildings not carefully designed for school purposes, and these buildings became infected and dangerous to the inmates. It is quite within the mark to say that fifty per cent of the children who passed through these schools did not live to benefit from the education which they had received therein.

It was only in the 1950s and '60s that the residential school system was gradually ended.

Day schools for Indians were eventually established but conditions did not improve quickly. It was not uncommon for teachers on Indian reserves to get half or less than half of the salary of their urban counterparts. This, of course, meant a high teacher turnover. Such conditions meant that many Indian people viewed education as a negative experience in their lives and avoided educational opportunities. Worse still, they did little to encourage their children, and probably discouraged them, in pursuing educational opportunities. The price which Canadian society is paying for this poor education is readily visible today.

Reserves

Besides the education system, there were many other ways in which the federal government tried to get Indians to give up the old ways. While Indians were not legally permitted to own reserve land on an individual basis, as early as 1869 the government introduced a system of pseudo-ownership of reserve land, to get Indian people to think of themselves as individual landowners. Thus the government developed a system of "location tickets" — an Indian would be given a parcel of property to occupy and given a location ticket for it. The system remains in place even today, though now in addition to "location tickets" the system has been refined to include certificates of possession and certificates of occupation. The idea behind this landholding scheme was that Indians would eventually want to give up their Indianness to become the individual owners of the land they occupied. The Indian Act even had a provision whereby a whole band could give up their Indian status and, presumably, become individual landowners. The process by which an Indian could give up his or her Indian status was called enfranchisement.

The irony was that while the government wanted Indians to become civilized (enfranchised), on the other hand it did not trust them. People were not allowed to decide that they were Indians, and thereby have the right to live in an Indian community on the reserve. The government felt it incumbent on itself to define who was an Indian. With the exception of Métis (in Alberta) no other Canadians have had the misfortune of having legislation define their racial or ethnic origin.

Indian Status

When colonial governments began creating reserves

in the early 1800s, they had to determine who could live on those reserves. The first such legislation was passed by Lower Canada (Quebec): it defined Indianness in sweeping terms, including all persons of Indian ancestry, all persons married to Indians, anyone adopted by Indians and living in his or her adopted community and finally anyone who was living with the band who was recognized by the band as being Indian. Shortly after the introduction of this law it was changed to provide that to be an Indian you had to be of Indian blood or alternatively show that at least your male predecessor was Indian. The law was also changed to provide that marriage only conferred status on non-Indian women, and not vice versa. This early legislation set a precedent for other colonial and later Dominion legislation. The first federal legislation in 1868 followed the definitions set out in the Lower Canada legislation. The concept of a wife's status being determined by her husband's was continued until 1985.

Early legislation also provided that when an Indian woman married she became a member of her husband's band and lost her membership in her own. This too continued in force until 1985. The male bias of the original legislation demonstrated European values. Many Eastern Canadian Indian societies were matriarchal. The Iroquois determined descent through the maternal line. Each family was ruled by a woman and chiefs selected for the Council of the Iroquois League first had to be approved by the matron of the family. This did not mean women were accepted as equal — decisions were still made by the male chiefs — but women were certainly powers behind the throne and membership was determined matrilineally.

Few Indian issues have created as much emotion, dissension and political rhetoric as the status issue. The Indian people naturally feel they are in the best position to decide whether or not they are Indians. The federal government, on the other hand, has long felt that it too has a legitimate interest in the issue: after all, Indians are recipients of considerable federal expenditure. In the last two decades much of the rhetoric centred on the controversial Indian Act provisions that made non-Indians of Indian women who married non-Indians. Of course, the same rules did not apply to Indian men; they could marry as they pleased without risk to their own status, and their wives legally became status Indians even if they had no Indian blood.

These discriminatory provisions were upheld by the Supreme Court of Canada in a 1973 decision that largely ignored John Diefenbaker's Canadian Bill of Rights. At issue was the status of two women; a Mrs. Lavell, whose name was struck off the Indian register because she had married a non-Indian, and a Mrs. Bedard, who was seeking to return to her Six Nations Reserve home after separation from her non-Indian husband.

These provisions became a *cause célèbre* with the feminist movement in the 1970s, and led to a condemnation of Canada by the United Nations Human Rights Committee, in 1981, after Sandra Lovelace of the Tobique Reserve in New Brunswick complained she was being denied the right to return to live on her home reserve after the break-up of her marriage to a non-Indian.

The discriminatory provisions were removed in 1985 after a prolonged and sometimes bitter debate, which climaxed with the anti-discrimination provisions receiving Royal Assent on June 26, 1985. (A similar

bill had died a year earlier when it was blocked in the
Senate.) Indian leaders (mostly male) took the view
that Parliament had no business defining who was an
Indian, and that only Indians could do that. Strong
statements were made by the bill's opponents. An
Alberta Indian chief told Parliament that they could
"expect violence...". Yet another Alberta Indian
leader, opposing the changes, warned that "...Another
Wounded Knee may result...It will cause bitterness,
hatred and division on the reserve." Another declared
that it didn't matter what the law said, "Those women
aren't welcome and won't be allowed on the reserve."
Several Alberta Indian organizations commenced a
court challenge to the legislation's constitutionality.

Feminists, human rights activists and native women's
groups took the position that it was unacceptable for
a law to treat women differently (worse) than men.
Indian leaders raised a valid issue — who should decide
who is an Indian? More was at stake than legal status
or cultural affiliation. Indian status carries with it a
host of benefits — the right to live on a reserve (which,
given the deplorable state of Indian housing, might
not always be a benefit), an exemption from taxation
(reserve income is not taxed and in some provinces
Indians are exempt from sales tax), health and education benefits. Status Indians receive funding for university education, including book costs, tuition fees, and
a living allowance (not always generous). Many opponents of the bill feared that these benefits would have
to be divided amongst more people. Many Alberta
Indians receive oil royalties and, not surprisingly, some
Alberta leaders feared having to share this with all the
reinstated Indians.

With Indian self-government likely to be a reality
in the next decade or two, Indian leaders argue that it

is crucial to any properly functioning government that the people governed be allowed to define who the members of that community are. As a model they point to the United States where Indian bands can pass bylaws dealing with band membership.

The 1985 changes to the Indian Act allow some Indian control over status. The federal government continues to have the right to decide whose names get on the Indian register. Bands can, however, by majority vote, decide to take control of band membership and establish their own rules for deciding who will be a part of the band.

This may lead to the creation of two types of Indians: those who are on the Indian register maintained by Ottawa but are not on any band list; and those who are on both the Indian list and the band list. Band membership might be significant as there could be certain benefits attached to it, such as sharing in oil or resource revenue. Band membership would also be necessary before one could live on the reserve and participate in band government.

Enfranchisement

Almost as quickly as governments passed legislation defining who was an Indian, laws were passed setting out how one could give up status. In 1857, the United Canadas (Upper and Lower) passed into law an Act for the Gradual Civilization of the Indian Tribes in the Canadas as a means of bringing Indians to full citizenship. That act empowered certain local authorities to report the case of any Indian who was

...of the male sex, and not under twenty-one years of age,...able to speak, read and write the English or

> French language readily and well, and is sufficiently advanced in the elementary branches of education and is of good moral character and free from debt...

to the governor who could then declare

> that such Indian is enfranchised under this Act; ...and...who shall no longer be deemed an Indian within the meaning thereof.

If a person met these criteria, he was placed on probation for one year, granted twenty hectares of land and after the year of probation was granted full citizenship. Ironically, if this standard had been applied to the white settlers of the time probably quite a number would have been disenfranchised for few of them were literate or free of debt. Not surprisingly only a handful of applicants applied for enfranchisement and only one application, that of Elias Hill, was accepted. Rather than re-examine the enfranchisement scheme, or ask whether Indians wanted to be civilized in this way, colonial officials blamed the failure of the scheme on Indian chiefs who, they claimed, discouraged their members from seeking the benefits of full citizenship. After all, some Indian leaders, like the Six Nations Council, had openly stated that they were "wholly averse to their people taking the advantages offered" by the act. The government's answer (by this time the federal government had been formed and had taken over responsibility for Indians) to this supposed rebellion was to introduce a new form of Indian government on Indian reserves.

The 1869 Act for the Gradual Enfranchisement of Indians gave the governor-in-council the power to impose elected municipal forms of government on

Indian bands. Chief and councillors were to be elected by all male members over the age of twenty-one years. The time, manner and place of election was to be determined by the superintendent of Indian affairs. Any elected official could be removed from office by the governor for dishonesty, intemperance or immorality. Whether the latter three had occurred was a matter for the sole determination of the governor-in-council. The act also set out what the elected council could do, which included making bylaws for order and decorum at public assemblies, public health, maintenance of roads and schools, the establishment of pounds, the prevention of trespass by cattle and the control of drinking. However, any action taken by the band council had to be approved by the governor-in-council. The 1869 law set a precedent for government interference in the selection of Indian chiefs and councillors that exists to this day. The 1876 Indian Act continued these rules as has every Indian Act since. It is only in recent times that some bands have reverted to electing chiefs and council by traditional means (essentially, chosen at a meeting and subject to removal at any time). The imposition of elected band councils was seen by government officials as a way of destroying the traditional Indian political system. Traditional elections are seen as a way of returning to it.

The 1869 act did little to speed up the process of enfranchisement and civilization. As a result, an even tougher law was passed in 1884, described as "An Act for conferring certain privileges on the more advanced bands of Canada with a view of training them for exercise of Municipal Affairs". This legislation too, had little effect.

The Conservative government of Arthur Meighen passed a law in 1920 that allowed the government to enfranchise Indians with or without their consent. The measure, however, was short-lived; it was repealed by Mackenzie King's Liberal government in 1922. While compulsory enfranchisement was done away with, the Indian Act continued to have provisions whereby Indians could voluntarily give up their status.

In the twenties, thirties and forties many Indians gave up their status so that they could go to school, drink or vote. (They got the right to vote federally in 1960; provincial laws giving Indians the right to vote and to drink in public establishments were changed during the 1950s and 1960s). Indians who went to university were actively encouraged to give up their Indian status. Indeed, for several decades, the only way to become a lawyer, doctor or priest was to give up your Indian status. During World War II and the Korean War many Indian servicemen were persuaded to accept enfranchisement; after all, if you were fighting for your country you might as well become a full citizen.

The push by the federal government to get Indians to give up their status continued into the 1960s. In 1969 the federal government, in its White Paper, proposed doing away with the Indian Act and Indian status. The paper concluded: ''The policies proposed recognize the simple reality that the separate legal status of Indians and the policies which have flowed from it have kept the Indian people apart from and behind other Canadians. The Indian people have not been full citizens of the communities and provinces in which they live and have not enjoyed the equality and benefits that such participation offers.''

Canada was not alone in this course of action. Between 1887 and 1934 the United States government adopted a policy of dividing tribal lands (owned by the Indian community as a whole) into individual parcels of 40, 80 or 160 acres and granting these parcels to individual Indians. Each parcel was held in trust by the U.S. government for twenty-five years, after which time title was granted to the Indian. Once the Indian was granted title he became a full citizen, entitled to vote and subject to the same laws as every other citizen. The theory behind this process was that an Indian who owned his own land would, automatically, become a farmer or rancher and that ownership of land would thus teach the Indian to be civilized and self-supporting. This process was in clear violation of the treaties the U.S. government had made with Indians, under which certain tracts of land were set aside for Indians. Almost 100 million acres of Indian land were parcelled in this manner. As with the Canadian experience the U.S. government found that this process did not turn Indians into farmers and eventually the policy was abandoned.

Canada officially gave up on enfranchisement in 1985. At that time the Indian Act was changed to allow those Indians who had given up their status, either to join Canada's armed forces, to go to school or to get a job, to regain their Indian status. And the enfranchisement provisions of the act were removed, making it impossible to give up status.

The Special Case of British Columbia

British Columbia was one jurisdiction where the implementation of the federal Indian policy of buying Indian lands never became reality. The colonies of Vancouver Island and British Columbia, unlike other early Canadian colonies, did not develop an Indian policy. In the late 1800s, when treaties were being signed on the prairies, the Indians in B.C. saw their rights being ignored; with the exception of a few treaties on Vancouver Island and the northeastern corner of the province, treaties with the Indians were not entered into either before or after British Columbia entered Confederation in 1871.

The colony of Vancouver Island was established by the British in 1849 on former Hudson's Bay Company lands. James Douglas, the company's chief factor in the area, became the first governor. Douglas stated that his policy was to "purchase the native rights in the land, in every case, prior to the settlement of any district", and at first he made a valiant attempt to live up to his policy. Between 1850 and 1854, Douglas signed fourteen treaties with Vancouver Island Indians, often obtaining the land for a few cents an acre or for a few blankets per acre. As part of these treaties, Douglas established several small reserves.

In 1858 the colony of British Columbia was established on the lower mainland, with Douglas again becoming governor. He had hoped to continue his policy of purchasing Indian land, but was unsuccessful for two reasons: first, he lacked the money to buy off the Indians; and second, the 1858 Cariboo gold rush made orderly development on mainland British Columbia impossible.

In his desire to reach treaties with the Indians Douglas was trying to carry out Colonial Office instructions. In 1858 he was instructed:

> I have to enjoin you to consider the best and most humane means of dealing with the Native Indians. The feelings of this country would be strongly opposed to the adoption of any arbitrary or oppressive measures towards them....Let me not omit to observe, that it

should be an invariable condition, in all bargains or treaties with the natives for the cession of lands possessed by them, that subsistence should be supplied to them in some other shape, and above all, that it is the earnest desire of Her Majesty's Government that your early attention should be given to the best means of diffusing the blessings of the Christian religion and of civilization among the natives.

To this Douglas replied:

...I made it a practice up to the year 1859, to purchase the native rights in the land, in every case prior to the settlement of any district; but since that time in consequence of the termination of the Hudson's Bay Company Charter, and the want of funds, it has not been in my power to continue it. Your Grace must indeed, be well aware that I have, since then, had the utmost difficulty in raising enough money to defray the most indispensable wants of Government.

The Colonial Office in London remained firm.

...the acquisition of the title is a purely colonial interest, and the Legislature must not entertain any expectation that the British taxpayer will be burthened to supply the funds or British credit pledged for the purpose.

The result was that Douglas let his policy of treating with the Indians lapse, and proceeded to issue a number of ordinances for settling and mining the land. He largely ignored the Indian land question though he did set aside several small reserves for Indians. His policy of at least paying lip service to Indian rights was officially shelved when he retired in 1864.

Responsibility for native policy was assumed by the commissioner of land and works, who stated, "The title of the Indians in fee of the public lands, or any portion thereof, has never been acknowledged by the Government, but on the contrary is distinctly denied." Under his tenure, British Columbia enacted a land ordinance giving 160 acres of free land to each settler family. Reserves for Indians on the other hand totalled ten acres per family. Further east on the prairies and in northern Ontario during that same period, the federal government was creating reserves of 160 and even 640 acres per family. Douglas's resignation and the implementation of the new policy even resulted in several violent incidents.

British Columbia entered Confederation in 1871. As in the rest of Canada the federal government undertook responsibility for Indians and Indian reserves. The colonial government agreed to transfer land required so the federal government could establish more reserves and pursue a policy "as liberal as that hitherto pursued by the British Columbia Government" (this latter wording appeared in the terms of union between B.C. and Canada). The irony was that in 1871 the policy of the colony of British Columbia was far from liberal in comparison with what was happening in the rest of Canada. The 1871 agreement fell apart even before it could be implemented. The federal government decided on a "reserve" policy of eighty acres in British Columbia but in 1874 the B.C. government adopted a land policy that made no provision for reserves. Under the British North America Act (and under today's Constitution) lands and resources belong to provincial governments. Therefore, the federal government could not simply take land and make a reserve. A compromise was reached in 1876 with the appointment of a joint Reserves Allotment Commission. British Columbia government support for the commission was less than heartfelt. After one commissioner resigned in frustration the commission finally got around to creating reserves in the 1880s.

The reserve creation process of the 1880s in B.C. was a haphazard one. Rather than resolving grievances it probably created more dissatisfaction in the Indian community. Most of the reserves created were small (in accordance with the B.C. policy on Indian reserves) and often the Indians, like the Nishga, who were accustomed to having the use of large areas of land found themselves confined to little plots. Often the reserves were created in areas the commission had not even visited; when visits were made they were likely to be very brief. There was no consultation with the Indians to establish what land they wanted for their reserves; surveyors appeared unannounced to survey lands. Indians who had built houses and tilled land found themselves threatened with eviction because the land on which they had located themselves was no longer an Indian reserve. Commercial fishing operations often appeared in traditional Indian fishing areas. Not surprisingly, such actions created resistance. Surveyors, settlers and fishermen were threatened and driven out. Indians organized and petitioned for recognition of Indian title. Often they were assisted by church missionaries.

A royal commission was appointed, the Royal Commission of Inquiry into the North-West Coast Indians, to investigate Indian discontent, particularly that of the Nishgas. Not surprisingly, the commission's findings resolved nothing. The provincial nominee was instructed to ''please be careful — while assuring the Indians that all they say will be reported to the proper authorities — not to give undertakings or make promises, and in particular you will be careful to discountenance, should it arise, any claim of Indian title to Provincial lands.'' The commission did just that.

This did not settle matters. Native agitation continued. A Nishga land committee was formed in 1890. Support for the Indian cause came from several Protestant churches. Several chiefs of the Squamish tribe drew up a petition stating that the title to their land had not been extinguished. A deputation of chiefs went to London and presented their grievances to King Edward VII. They were told that they should try to settle their grievances with the Canadian government, and politely sent on their way. Yet another royal commission was appointed in 1913 to deal with the issue of Indian reserves in British Columbia. Three years later the McKenna-McBride Commission recommended a decrease in the size of existing reserves by over 47,000 acres and the addition of 87,000 acres of other land for Indian reserves. While the report was accepted by the two governments the Indians refused to accept it. They asked that the issue of aboriginal rights be referred to the Privy Council in London (at that time the final court of appeal for Canada.) The governments refused. The matter was instead referred to a parliamentary committee set up to inquire into the state of Indian title in B.C. In 1927 that committee reported that

> Having given full and careful consideration to all that was adduced before your committee, it is the unanimous opinion of the members thereof, that the petitioners have not established any claim to the lands of British Columbia based on aboriginal or other title…it is the further opinion of your committee that the matter should now be regarded as finally closed.

Lest there be any doubt about the B.C. land issue being closed the federal government made it an offence to pursue Indian land claims. That same year the federal government passed section 141 of the Indian Act, which stated

> Every person, who…receives, obtains, solicits or requests from any Indian any payment or contribution for the purpose of raising a fund or providing money for the prosecution of any claim which the tribe or band of Indians to which such Indian belongs, or of which he is a member, has or is represented to have for the recovery of any claim or money for the benefit of the said tribe or band, shall be guilty of an offence…

The land claims prohibition remained on the statute books until 1951.

The legacy of these B.C. policies is still evident in Canada today. British Columbia continues to refuse recognition of Indian land rights. Because of its strong opposition, it is from B.C. that a number of precedent-setting court decisions have arisen, including the Nishga land claims case (*Calder* v. *Attorney General of British Columbia*), Meares Island, the South Moresby Islands, the double-tracking case and the Musqueam case. B.C. Indians have been forced to look to the courts for help in gaining recognition of their land rights. And in some cases, the Haida on Queen Charlotte Islands have physically blocked logging operations, defying the courts.

The B.C. stand has been equally visible at recent constitutional conferences on aboriginal rights. The B.C. government was one of the adamant opponents of entrenching Indian self-government in the Constitution when the subject was discussed in the 1983, 1984 and 1985 constitutional conferences.

In 1984 the federal government took a first step in trying to correct some of the injustices B.C. Indians have suffered. It passed legislation to allow for negotiations to restore reserve lands that had been taken away, in particular by the McKenna-McBride Commission.

Broken Treaties

It was not only in B.C. that lands reserved for Indian reserves have been taken away by the government; this has occurred even when the lands had been set aside by treaty. The prairies are a good example of how the Indian Affairs bureaucracy in the early 1900s took treaty lands. When prairie treaties were signed the country was virtually uninhabited, and little attention was paid to the location and size of the reserves. But as the prairies were opened up settlers, speculators and government officials realized that some choice land had been given up to Indians. In the late 1800s and early 1900s government officials began to actively encourage Indians to give up their reserves. Provision had been made in federal legislation dating back to 1868 for Indians to give up their reserves, and it is still part of Indian Act legislation. A basic stipulation throughout that time was and is that, for a surrender of an Indian reserve to be valid, it must be approved by a majority vote at a public meeting held for the purpose of approving the surrender.

Perhaps the best statement of the view the government took of lands it had given in the west for Indian reserves can be found in the 1908 annual report by the deputy superintendent general of Indian affairs wherein he stated:

So long as no particular harm nor inconvenience accrued from the Indians' holding vacant lands out of proportion to their requirements, and no profitable disposition thereof was possible, the department firmly opposed any attempt to induce them to divest themselves of any part of their reserves.

Conditions, however, have changed and it is now recognized that where Indians are holding tracts of farming or timber lands beyond their possible requirements and by doing so seriously impeding the growth of settlement, and there is such demand as to ensure profitable sale...it is in the best interests of all concerned to encourage such sales.

Indian organizations allege that various fraudulent practices were used by departmental officials in order to get Indians to surrender good reserve land, which the department felt could be put to better use. The Indian Act required that all surrenders had to be approved by the majority of the band. Allegations are that officials often used threats against bands to get them to agree to surrenders. Sometimes they falsely reported results of meetings (alleging that a surrender had been approved when in fact it had not) and sometimes reports were filed by departmental officials indicating that meetings approving surrenders had taken place, when they had not. Sometimes, it was departmental officials themselves who benefited from these surrenders, by buying and speculating in the land.

In one well-documented case, 220 Assiniboines were moved off the Pheasant's Rump and Ocean Man Reserves and settled among the Cree of the White Bear Reserve. The land was bought by three high-ranking departmental officials for the purpose of speculating in it. At the 1901 surrender meeting, the Assiniboines were told that if they didn't move voluntarily they would be forced out by the police. The Liberal government of John Turner accepted that the federal government had defrauded the Assiniboine in 1901 and announced a settlement of $19 million. The Federation of Saskatchewan Indian Nations alleges that Indians in Saskatchewan alone were defrauded of some 416,000 acres of reserve land during the twenty-year period 1890-1910.

Not only reserves on the prairies were taken. In 1911 the Indian Act was amended to allow Indians to be dispossessed of reserves that were located near urban centres. The act permitted the government to order a judicial inquiry to determine whether Indians on reserves near urban centres should be removed from the reserve for the public interest.

Native People in Newfoundland

While the Indians of British Columbia and the prairies certainly have their problems the Indians of Newfoundland not only have been unsuccessful in having any land rights recognized but are not even considered Indians. No treaties or reserves have ever been set aside for Indians and Inuit in Labrador and Newfoundland. Mainland Newfoundland was inhabited by some 500 Beothuks when Cabot first saw Newfoundland shores. The last Beothuk died in 1829. Considerable controversy surrounds the disappearance of the Beothuk. Were they destroyed by the Micmacs who were encouraged by the French, or were they hunted down by English sailors? In the 1800s several tribes of Micmac, Montagnais, Naskapi and Malecite Indians migrated to Newfoundland, where at the time there were no policies for dealing with the Indians. In 1949, when Newfoundland joined Canada, the terms of union were silent about Indians. Since then the federal government has undertaken some responsibility for some Indians in Newfoundland but has been reluctant to recognize them as status Indians. As a result Newfoundland Indians have been forced to take action to gain recognition. For example, the Indians of Conne River have had to occupy federal buildings and sue in court to try and gain Indian status. Eventually, they achieved some success when the federal government recognized them as Indians; however, they are still fighting to have their traditional lands recognized as an Indian reserve. They are in much the same situation as the Métis, who are also fighting for government recognition of their status as aboriginal people of Canada.

6
The Métis

They live in towns with names like Camperville, Manitoba; Duck Lake, Saskatchewan; and Big Prairie, Alberta, and like other native people they have started to move to urban centres. Some of their names are French-sounding and some have Scottish names. Michif is the language which some of them still speak. These are the people of the Métis nation. To get satisfaction for their grievances they formed their own government twice in the 1800s. On one of those occasions they helped bring about the formation of a new province, Manitoba; but they soon found themselves a minority in that province.

Métis is a French word meaning half-breed. During the settlement of Canada there was a perpetual shortage of European women. This, coupled with the fact that many soldiers and traders, sent to Canada on short-term assignment, established temporary liaisons which they then left behind, meant the growth of a mixed-blood population. For the most part, until well into the 1800s, these people were absorbed into the Indian community. Matters developed differently in western Canada. Thanks to their common grievances against the Hudson's Bay Company, the political consciousness of the mixed-blood population of the Red River Valley grew. Political unity was possible because the Red River Valley Métis had developed organizations — for the buffalo hunt — that they were then able to use to advance their grievances against the company.

The word *Métis* can be used in two senses. First, to refer to anyone of mixed blood. However, the more historically correct reference is to those people of western Canada of mixed-blood origin who united to protest their grievances and treatment at the hands of first the Hudson's Bay Company and later the Canadian government.

The Métis of western Canada are unique; there are almost no other mixed-blood populations in the world who have developed a political and cultural consciousness. The Métis are not Indians; their culture, language and political aspirations make them a people apart. What they do share with the Indians is poverty and the same inconsistency and uncertainty regarding government policy.

The Métis nation grew out of the fur trade in the northwest. Two rival companies, the Hudson's Bay Company (based in England) and the North West Company (based in Montreal) competed for furs in western Canada. The Hudson's Bay Company was formed in 1670 and the North West in the 1760s.

At first, the London headquarters of the Hudson's Bay Company forbade liaisons between its traders and Indian women. Headquarters thought that Indian women in company forts would pose a security risk. That rule was the most frequently broken of all the company rules, and eventually headquarters relented: even company officers were forming liaisons with Indian women. The Scottish employees of the company were certainly lonely and wanted feminine companionship, but besides that they needed to be taught how to survive in the harsh, rugged Hudson's Bay area. Indian women knew how to snare rabbits with willow twigs, how to chew moosehide into moccasins and how to prepare furs. In short, a man with an Indian wife had qualified local help to survive the prairie climate. For a trader, an Indian wife also meant having a contact in the Indian community, a valuable commercial lead. It also meant protection from being harassed by the Indian community. The advantages were not all one-sided. For the Indian community, having a member of the band married to a trader meant having a contact in the commercial world.

While these liaisons were not marriages in the European sense, they were usually entered upon with the consent of the woman's family. At least one such union was held to be a valid marriage by the courts of Quebec: in 1803 one William Connolly took an Indian woman and lived with her for twenty-eight years; they had six children. The court ruled that the man's second marriage, upon his return to Quebec, was invalid and the offspring from the first marriage were entitled to his property.

The sad thing about all these liaisons was that at the end of their term of service the Bay men returned to England or Scotland, leaving behind their wives and offspring. The wives were left to the upkeep of the tribe, or found other trader husbands.

The pattern followed by the Montreal traders was different. The French traders tended to establish more permanent roots in their areas of operation. Unlike the Hudson's Bay men, most were not working on term appointments. They erected waterfront log cabins and cultivated garden plots. Indian women were taken as wives, and soon there was a significant population that was neither French nor Indian. In fact, there was a minor population boom. One North West trader, Alexander Henry, estimated in 1805 that there were 1,090 North West traders who had 368 wives and 569 children. In his own post he had 36 traders, 27 wives and

67 children. This phenomenal population growth even prompted the North West Company to ban marriages with Indian women; only Métis women could be married.

The offspring of these liaisons became a people in their own right; neither French nor Indian. To at least one British civil servant, Herman Merivale (a university professor when he made the comment, he later became permanent undersecretary at the Colonial Office), the growth of the half-breed culture was proof that through intermarriage the Indian could be amalgamated into the Canadian mainstream.

The Métis became guides, interpreters and message carriers for the fur trading companies. More importantly, they quickly became frontier traders themselves; acting as middlemen between the western Indians and the trading companies. They also played a significant role in negotiating treaties with Indians on the prairies and in northwestern Ontario.

The Rise of the Métis Nation

It was the challenge to their fur-trade role and their way of life that gave birth to Métis nationalism. The first such challenge culminated in June 1816 with what some historians mistakenly label the Massacre of Seven Oaks. The story started several years earlier, when Lord Selkirk became concerned about the economic plight of his Scottish countrymen. His answer was emigration; he decided to establish a colony in the Red River Valley. Selkirk was able to buy 116,000 square miles (approximately 300,000 square kilometres) in the Red River area from the Hudson's Bay Company. There was no consultation with people living in the area, who for the most part were Métis traders and hunters. To complicate matters, many of the Métis were in the employ of the North West Company, which was openly hostile to the settlement.

Tensions between the traders and the settlers grew. The Métis were prohibited from running buffalo out of the area by the colony's governor, and some of their pemmican was seized. In return, the North West Company encouraged young Métis men to harass the colonists. In the summer of 1815 they raided some of the colonists' farms. In May of 1816, the Métis captured the Hudson's Bay Company pemmican boats on the Qu'Appelle River, then plundered Brandon House, a Hudson's Bay Company post. The Métis then sought to move the pemmican to Lake Winnipeg so it could be shipped to North West posts on the prairies (the Saskatchewan River, which flows to Hudson's Bay via the north end of Lake Winnipeg, was a major water route into western Canada). To get to Lake Winnipeg they had to skirt the Selkirk colony. The colony's governor, on hearing of the proximity of the Métis, took a party of twenty men to find out what they were up to and to assert his authority over the area.

The two groups met in a shady group of trees known as Seven Oaks. A messenger rode from the Métis camp asking the governor to either surrender or be fired upon. The governor tried to grab the messenger's gun and reins; the messenger fell from his horse, and shots were exchanged. Both sides went into action. By nightfall twenty-one settlers and one Métis were dead.

The Battle of Seven Oaks did not sound the death knell for the colony. Military reinforcements arrived to protect the colony and legal proceedings were taken against the North West Company. While the battle did not mean the death of the colony it did give rise to the Métis nation. This was the first time the Métis had united to protect a way of life and had achieved some success.

Métis nationalism continued to grow, thanks to the Hudson's Bay Company. Aside from the buffalo hunt the major employment in the area was fur trading. (Though it should be pointed out that not all Métis were hunters or traders — some became wealthy merchants). The North West was taken over by the Bay in 1821, thereby leaving the Bay with a monopoly. Almost without exception the Métis were excluded from the officer ranks of the Bay and were limited to labouring jobs. Officers continued to be imported. The only way a Métis could get ahead was to become an independent trader. Free traders could acquire goods and dispose of furs on the American side of the border. This however, contravened the Bay's legal monopoly.

In 1849 the company charged four Métis with contravening the monopoly. May 17 was the trial date. The first to be tried was one Pierre-Guillaume Sayer. The Métis organized into an informal self-defence league. The evidence was clear that Sayers had traded whisky for furs and had broken the company's monopoly. The jury, after finding Sayer guilty, recommended mercy; the court agreed, and Sayer was released after being admonished by the judge. The company dropped charges against Sayer's three other companions. When Sayer emerged from the courthouse announcing that he had been released the crowd roared "*Vive la liberté! La commerce est libre!*"

The Manitoba Rebellion of 1869-1870

Thus, by 1869, the Métis had been welded into a politically conscious people. They had had experience in fighting for their rights and had achieved some success in protecting their way of life. While Louis Riel is often regarded as the catalyst who sparked the rebellion, the political climate was ripe for it, even without Riel's leadership.

Problems began almost immediately after Confederation in 1867, when the federal government began to negotiate for the transfer of Hudson's Bay Company lands to the new Dominion. This made the Métis angry. They had developed small trading enterprises and farms on river lots, and the transfer to the Dominion government scared them: what would happen to their lands and lifestyle? The Métis took the view that the Hudson's Bay Company could sell the federal government its trading monopoly — nothing more. Land rights could not be sold to the government, because the company did not own the land; it belonged to the Indians and the Métis and had to be acquired from them.

Essentially all the Métis wanted in 1869 was a government guarantee that their rights would be protected. Unfortunately, the federal government ignored the inhabitants. Negotiations were concluded in 1869 between England, Canada and the Hudson's Bay Company for the transfer of Rupert's Land and the Northwest Territory.

A federal government survey party arrived in Manitoba in the fall of 1869. On October 11, 1869, Riel and a large group of Métis challenged the right of the survey party to cross land belonging to one André Nault. Again a victory for the Métis — the surveyors withdrew. Two weeks later, the Métis formed a National Committee and blocked the road to the United States thus preventing the lieutenant-governor-designate (appointed to rule over the territory) from entering the territory. Upper Fort Garry was seized by the Métis on November 2, 1869, and several weeks later on

December 8, 1869, Riel declared his provisional government by issuing the Declaration of the People of Rupert's Land and the North-West.

In Riel's view his actions were perfectly within the law for three reasons. First, he took the position that God creates tribes of people and in doing so must place them somewhere. He had created Indians and the Métis and had given them the Canadian prairies. Their rights could only be acquired by purchase. Second, when Canada paid £300,000 (English pounds) to the Hudson's Bay Company in 1869 for Rupert's Land, this payment was only to buy out the company's trading monopoly, not to buy the land, because the company had no right to the land. Third, Riel argued that the only legitimate government over the Red River area was the Hudson's Bay Company (it had that right by charter). When it abandoned the area a void was created, and the people had the right to form their own government. Further, Riel argued that in international law people could not be transferred from one legal government to another without their consent.

The Riel government (as again in 1885) was not supported by all the Métis. At the same time it did have support from some other settlers and traders who were not entirely happy with the way Ottawa was proceeding with the acquisition of the West. There is more than a grain of truth to the suggestion that Riel was the first to voice western concerns about Ottawa's treatment of the west.

Riel's government spent much of its time drawing up the list of its demands and the conditions on which it would enter Confederation. The fact that Riel and the Métis always saw themselves as being a part of Canada is often overlooked — they simply wanted assurance that Canada would respect their property rights, their culture and language. Not surprisingly, some people have suggested that Riel should be viewed as one of the Fathers of Confederation.

During the winter of 1870 considerable energy was expended in defining the community's demands and conditions. There is still considerable historical debate about the extent of community agreement at the time the three delegates of the provisional government were sent to Ottawa to negotiate. Generally speaking, those demands could be summarized as being provincehood, language rights (the root of much of the debate about French-language rights in Manitoba today), protection of land and property rights and a general amnesty for the events of 1869-70 (on March 4, 1870, a troublesome Ontario labourer, Thomas Scott, had been executed by the provisional government).

When they arrived in Ottawa, the delegates from the Red River were treated with a signal lack of respect: they were arrested and thrown in jail. Eventually they were let out, and met with members of the federal cabinet to negotiate the entry of Manitoba into Confederation. Those terms became the Manitoba Act which received Royal Assent on May 12 and became effective July 15, 1870. The act met many of the Métis demands — it granted provincehood, created bilingual institutions and purportedly guaranteed Métis property rights. The Manitoba Act, however, covered only a hundred square miles — the rest of the Canadian prairies became the Northwest Territories, governed separately from Manitoba.

Riel saw the Manitoba Act and the oral assurance of amnesty as an international treaty between two independent nations. If one nation broke its part of the deal, the other was no longer bound by it. The provisional government even took a vote on the Manitoba

Act, and after the vote Riel wrote to the Canadian secretary of state accepting the terms of union on behalf of the Provisional Government. As Riel found out when he went to Ottawa to represent Manitoba in Parliament, he was a wanted man and the assurances of amnesty were meaningless. The guarantee of Métis land rights was equally worthless. The message from Ottawa was clear, and in spite of the settlement reached by the Manitoba Act, the army kept marching westward, reaching Manitoba one week before the civilian lieutenant-governor who had been appointed to govern Manitoba.

At the time of its entry into Confederation Manitoba had a population of 12,000, 10,000 of whom were Métis. Many of the Métis had settled along the river; sometimes they had obtained legal permission from the Hudson's Bay Company and sometimes they had simply chosen a site, and settled there. The Manitoba Act had two guarantees for the Métis. First, it provided that 1.4 million acres (one-seventh of the total area of Manitoba at the time) would be granted to the Métis in order to extinguish ''the Indian Title...of the half-breed residents''. Second, the act guaranteed that those Métis already in possession of land would be left in peaceful possession of that land.

While these protections were contained in the Manitoba Act they were probably practised more in the breach. And when necessary the law was changed in order to conform with the practice. Between 1873 and 1884 the law dealing with Métis lands in Manitoba was changed no fewer than eleven times. One historian has argued that many of these changes were unconstitutional because the amendment to the British North America Act in 1871 declared that the Canadian Parliament was not authorized to change the Manitoba Act.

What rights were guaranteed? First, a total of 1.4 million acres of land was to be given to the Métis to buy out their "Indian title". Section 31 of the Manitoba Act stated:

> And whereas, it is expedient, towards the extinguishment of the Indian Title to the lands in the Province, to appropriate a portion of such ungranted lands, to the extent of one million four hundred thousand acres thereof, for the benefit of the families of the half-breed residents, it is hereby enacted that...the Lieutenant-Governor shall select such lots or tracts in such parts of the Province as he may deem expedient, to the extent aforesaid, and divide the same among the children of the half-breed heads of families residing in the Province...

Governor Archibald, the province's first lieutenant-governor, read this section as meaning that 1.4 million acres of land was to be conferred by him on all mixed-blood people, women, men or children. His superior, Joseph Howe, federal secretary of state for the provinces, told Archibald not to give "countenance to the wholesale appropriation of large tracts of country by halfbreeds" and instructed Archibald to stay out of the half-breed land question. 1873 saw the first change to the Manitoba Act — it was made clear that the recipients of the 1.4 million acres were to be half-breed children, not heads of families. This had the effect of reducing the number of beneficiaries from 10,000 to less than 6,000. A year later the law was changed again — heads of families were offered scrip, a piece of paper which was supposed to be redeemable for land.

The scrip system was later extended to other parts of the northwest. It also gave rise to land speculation and fraud. Land speculators often happened, conveniently, to be around when scrip was issued, with the result that many Métis signed over their land titles and scrip to speculators, often for nominal compensation. Looking through old Dominion land records one finds that title to many parcels of Métis land was often issued to the same person. It has even been alleged that the land or scrip was never even issued to the Métis, but issued directly to land speculators. Perhaps in an effort to destroy evidence, hundreds of assignments of scrip were mysteriously destroyed in a fire while being shipped to Ottawa during the early 1870s. On three occasions, in 1873, 1874 and 1885, the Manitoba government passed laws providing that no matter what irregularities had occurred in the assignment of scrip or Métis lands the title of the current holder was unassailable.

One million four hundred thousand acres had been promised to Manitoba's 10,000 Métis; and the promise was constitutionally enshrined in the Manitoba Act. By 1886, all of the 1.4 million acres had been allotted through more than 5,000 land grants. Less than a thousand Métis still owned parts of the 1.4 million acres — the rest was in the hands of speculators or purchasers who had acquired from speculators.

The Métis were no more successful in hanging on to the land that they already had in their possession at the time Manitoba entered Confederation. Section 32 of the Manitoba Act guaranteed that anyone who had obtained title or permission to settle land from the Hudson's Bay Company would be given title by the government. The section also guaranteed that people who were in peaceful possession of land, no matter how they had taken possession, would be guaranteed title to the land. Many Métis simply took up winter residence (in the summer they were usually out on the buffalo hunt) along one of the rivers in Manitoba, without seeking permission from the Hudson's Bay Company. Section 32 of the Manitoba Act also guaranteed certain rights to the haylots.

After surveying Manitoba, the government advertised in the newspaper that people claiming under section 32 could come forward to press their claims. However, matters were almost immediately complicated by the government's opening up of Manitoba for homesteading even before it had completed its survey and determined what rights the Métis settlers had. As a result, longtime Métis residents often found new arrivals on their land.

Another difficulty that arose was that the surveyors often classified a lot as vacant if the land was not cultivated and if permanent buildings had not been erected on it. The government took the position that improvements had to exist on the land before it would recognize ownership (this was in fact a departure from the Manitoba Act, which promised title on the basis of simple possession). The requirement of improvements to the land had to be proved by the surveyor's certificate, with the surveyor having absolute discretion in deciding whether the improvements were sufficient.

To make it even more difficult, applications were first screened locally, then sent to Ottawa. More than one application became bogged down in bureaucracy. At one point the federal Senate proposed that claims should be dealt with in open court or by a quasi-judicial body but the government refused, saying claims could be dealt with more expeditiously by the bureaucracy. Further breaches of the Manitoba Act occurred when portions of the riverlots and adjoining haylands were expropriated without compensation (by special legislation).

Behind all the bureaucratic and legal manoeuvering was an attempt to keep Métis off the river lots and out of Manitoba. That was succinctly stated by Interior Minister David Laird in the Liberal administration of 1873-78. Laird feared that indiscriminate recognition of rights under section 32 would lead to too great a concentration of half-breeds in the settlement belt. He preferred to see the Métis displaced from their river lots and moved to the north where they could become fishermen and labourers.

Matters for the Métis claimants were even further complicated by fraud, which was being perpetrated by a senior Ottawa official responsible for processing Métis claims. After claims were dealt with in Winnipeg (not all claims made it through the Manitoba bureaucracy) they were forwarded to Ottawa. One Robert Lang was responsible for preparing files for final scrutiny in Ottawa. He selected those files that had the strongest likelihood of success (they met the requirements of law) and advised his Manitoba associates, A. Mathewman and A.G.B. Bannatyne, of these claims. His Manitoba associates visited the claimant informing him that his claim was quite weak but if he provided extra information to their man in Ottawa the obstacles could be cleared. The price was half of the claimant's land. After the conspiracy was discovered, Lang fled the country. The federal Justice Department declared that Lang's offence was not extraditable. To prevent a public scandal, the government decided that it was under no obligation to do anything about these conspiracies because they had been directed not against the government but against private individuals. It was up to the individuals to take legal action against the conspirators.

David Laird's objective of driving out the Métis was achieved by this legal, political, bureaucratic and criminal manoeuvering. Less than 20 per cent of the Métis occupying river lots actually got title to their land. The loss of land, coupled with a decline in buffalo herds in Manitoba, forced many of the Métis westward. While the Métis of Manitoba had negotiated guarantees for their rights before entering Confederation, by 1886 the Métis formed a mere 7 per cent of the population of Manitoba. Some moved and the rest were swamped in a sea of non-Métis immigrants. Of those who moved some went to the Batoche area, where in 1885 they would be faced with many of the same difficulties and challenges they had faced in Manitoba.

The Scrip System

The system of Métis land grants was extended to the Northwest Territories in 1879 by federal legislation. However, after passage of the law, nothing happened for several years. Métis complaints and the Northwest Rebellion of 1885 finally brought about some action. In January 1885 the federal government established a commission to enumerate Métis in the Northwest Territories who had been born before July 15, 1870 (originally those were the only. Métis entitled to land scrip, though it was later extended to include other Métis). In March, the commission was authorized to issue land and money scrip. In April the amount of scrip was established, being 240 acres or $240 for children and 160 or $160 for heads of families. In the next three years 3,446 Métis claims were allowed.

Lest these provisions be seen as being extremely generous it should be remembered that under the homestead policy established by the federal government 160 acres was granted for a nominal fee to any settler who made improvements to the land. Thus the Métis were really not getting much more than any other settler even though they had a greater claim to property in the west. As in Manitoba, few Métis saw either land or fair payment for land. The same speculative practices that had deprived the Métis of their land rights in Manitoba moved westward.

The extent of the abuses has been documented by the Alberta Métis Association in their book, *Métis Land Rights in Alberta: A Political History*. One R.A. Rutlan of the Edmonton Dominion Lands Office wrote in 1896 to the commissioner of Dominion lands in Winnipeg, expressing concern over the use of powers of attorney by speculators. According to him

> Brokers hoping to make money out of the scrip are agitating for a supplemental grant. They hope to excite the Half-Breed to an interest in the matter by agreeing to purchase; their expectation is probably that if Half-Breed [sic] move strongly the Government will yield. In the meanwhile the brokers are getting these powers of Attorney signed by the prospective beneficiaries. To the execution of the instrument the Half-Breed will be lured by an assurance that it is a 'petition' or 'Census form'. He will be told he will get his share of scrip if the Government issues it — I daresay the present process is much like the old one under which these people were swindled right and left and everywhere to the fullest extent. I do not believe that the Métis allottee benefitted to the extent of 20% of the original grant.

It should be remembered that many Métis could not read and write; others were fluent in French or Michif and not English. Therefore, it comes as no surprise that many were tricked into signing away their rights.

J.A. Gregory, who later became a Saskatchewan M.L.A., described the scrip process in the following terms:

> ...the Half-Breed was taken by the speculator who had purchased his scrip to the most convenient or most complaisant Dominion Land Agent in certain districts. The necessary affadavits [sic] were administered to him, but the actual descriptions of land were left blank to be filled in at the convenience of the speculator, who then had only to apply the scrip upon whatever piece of available land he desired, and then make application to the government for title which was issued in due course. There was little secret about these practices.

Father Lacombe, a well-known Catholic missionary, wrote to the Winnipeg Free Press in 1896 with the same complaint.

> The law of the land would not permit a man to retain property taken from a minor; but it allows sharks to use legal devices to rob unwary people of their property. No sooner did it become known that the government of Canada contemplated issuing scrip to half-breeds, than the sharks set to work to devise safe means to rob them.

Speculation defeated much of the legitimate Métis claim to land in western Canada. Whether the federal government knew and turned a blind eye to the practice still remains uncertain.

The North-West Rebellion of 1885

By 1885 some 1,500 Métis had established villages and a stable community on the banks of the South Saskatchewan River; the centre of their settlement was Batoche. There were mills, churches, stores, poolrooms and almost everything else one could find in a small community.

Batoche and the surrounding area was included in the first federal survey of the prairies, carried out between 1871 and 1879. Most of the land agents and surveyors spoke no French and at best were reluctant to tell the Métis whether the government would recognize their property rights (they were probably in no position to do so).

It was such concerns that led to the announcement of a Métis provisional government on March 19, 1885. The popular view of Canadian history is that this independence declaration was the result of Louis Riel's leadership. To complicate matters, in recent years some historians have spent considerable energy debating whether Riel was a sane man in 1885, and the idea has been fostered that the North-West Rebellion was the creation of an insane charismatic leader. Whether Riel was sane or insane is irrelevant. The issue is that in the 1880s there was considerable dissatisfaction in western Canada, not only among the Métis but also among whites and Indians, about Ottawa's treatment of legitimate western grievances.

In the 1880s Canada was touched by an economic depression. Western Indians were particularly affected by the austerity measures adopted to cope with the depression. Edgar Dewdney, lieutenant-governor of the Northwest Territories, made a severe cut in Indian rations at a time when the buffalo herds were vanishing, and not surprisingly, starvation was commonplace amongst Indian communities. At the same time, Indians were finding themselves, as a result of treaties signed in the 1870s, confined to the reserves. They found reserve life much less than they had expected. Indian leaders began to agitate for a renegotiation of the treaties.

White settlers were equally unhappy with their lot. Their concerns included a lack of representative government, the high cost of shipping goods to the west, and the cost of manufactured goods. Newspaper editorials in the Edmonton *Bulletin* and the Prince Albert *Times* suggested that a rebellion was necessary to make Ottawa pay attention to western concerns.

The Métis of Batoche collaborated with the whites in Prince Albert in forwarding complaints to Ottawa. (The two communities are approximately forty kilometres apart). A first meeting was held between the two groups in the spring of 1884. The western protesters forwarded a list of grievances to Ottawa on December 16, 1884, asking for representation in government, provincial status, recognition of Métis and Indian rights and a railway to Hudson Bay. Ottawa dismissed the petition, claiming that the economic situation prevented the government from undertaking any type of program that required the expenditure of money.

At the same time, Métis leaders were also having discussions with various Indian leaders. They hoped that with a united front (Métis, Indians, whites) Ottawa would move.

Ottawa refused to budge. The Métis declared a provisional government on March 19, 1885, which lasted until May 12, when it suffered military defeat at the hands of the Canadian army. Not all Métis joined the cause. In fact, Francois-Xavier Letendre collected over $19,000 from the Rebellion Losses Commission for losses he had suffered during the rebellion. There were many other Métis who did not support the provisional government and looked for other ways of settling their grievances.

Once the rebellion started, Ottawa quickly found the $5 million needed to fight the rebellion, and also found the money needed to complete the building of the CPR.

The rebellion had a number of other consequences for Indian and Métis rights. Within days of the outbreak of violence, Macdonald ordered an increase in rations for Indians. Soon, greatly increased quantities of flour, bacon, tea and tobacco were flowing to the Indian reserves. However, the rebellion also led to the institution of the pass system; and the military defeat of the Métis and their Indian supporters meant the government no longer had to worry about Indian complaints about their treaties and reserves.

Eighteen eighty-five also marked the beginning of the government scrip system. In 1879 the Dominion Lands Act was amended to extend the system to the northwest. However, it was only the threat of rebellion which finally forced the government to do something about it.

The rebellion also meant the further dispersal of the Métis. Some went to the United States (Montana and the Dakotas), others fled to northern Alberta and Saskatchewan communities like Battle River, Green Lake, Lac Ste. Anne, Lac La Biche and St. Paul de Métis. Of course, there were Métis who remained in the Batoche area.

Perhaps the most important consequence of the North-West Rebellion was the destruction of Métis nationhood. It would be a long time before any Métis group seriously advanced Métis land claims again. In 1885 the Métis had been crushed militarily and the government saw no need to concern itself with their claims. But the land rights issue did not vanish with the defeat at Batoche. It remained dormant until it surfaced again in Alberta forty-five years later. Of course, there were Métis activists but the defeats of the late 1800s made political organization difficult. To complicate matters most Métis found themselves living in extreme poverty.

The Alberta Métis Colonies

In 1895, the Catholic Church leased federal land at St. Paul de Métis (now St. Paul, Alberta) to start a Métis colony. Fifteen years later the colony failed but the example inspired other colonies. In the decades that followed many Métis simply squatted on land in northern Alberta and continued to live a partially settled and partially nomadic life. Often they grouped together in small settlements.

The 1920s and 1930s saw the government move to open more land for settlement, particularly land in northern and central Alberta, some of it land on which the Métis were living. Uncertainty about their land led the Métis to become politically active again.

Coupled with land concerns, many Alberta Métis, like Métis elsewhere, were finding themselves living in destitute circumstances. Over 80 per cent of the adults were illiterate and it was estimated that over 90 per cent had been infected with tuberculosis.

The Alberta Métis first met as a group in 1930 thanks to the efforts of one Joe Dion. He was later joined in his organizational efforts by Jim Brady and Malcolm Norris. Their efforts eventually led to the formation of the first Alberta Métis organization, L'Association des Métis d'Alberta et des Territoires des Nord Ouest, in 1932.

In February, 1933, thanks in part to the work of the new organization, the Métis situation was discussed in the Alberta legislature. Premier Brownlee, for the United Farmers Association government, in response to opposition queries said that the Métis "problem" was not just a provincial responsibility but also a federal responsibility. The legislature eventually adopted a resolution that the government "...keeping...in mind the health, education, relief and general welfare of the half-breed population, continue its study and enquiry into the problems and present its recommendations to this assembly within ten days of the commencement of the next session thereof."

The resolution generated some internal government discussion of the Métis situation, including a civil servant's report that reserves should be set aside for Métis. The government, however, did little; it was waiting for the federal government to assume some or all of the responsibility for the Métis. So when the Alberta legislature met in the spring of 1934 nothing had been done. Métis leaders were pressing for the establishment of reserves — they were arguing that Métis land claims had never been satisfied and that the setting aside of reserves was a way of settling Métis land claims. A new motion was passed in the spring session of 1934, committing the Alberta government to an impartial study of the Métis situation. Things, however, did not move very quickly. Not only was the provincial government waiting for Ottawa to take responsibility, but the UFA government itself was in disarray. Finally, on July 17, 1934, the provincial cabinet voted to establish a royal commission to study the Métis question.

The appointment of commissioners was delayed until December — the Alberta government was hoping that Ottawa would agree to name at least one commissioner. Ottawa maintained (and still does) that Métis were a provincial responsibility and that Métis land claims were settled under the Manitoba Act and the scrip system under the Dominion Lands Act.

The terms of reference made clear that the commission, chaired by Judge Ewing, a judge of the Alberta Supreme Court, was to focus on issues concerning health, education, relief and the general welfare of the Métis. No reference was made to Métis land rights. In response to Malcolm Norris's arguments about Métis self-determination, Judge Ewing stated that he didn't see much reason for raking up past mistakes and was more concerned about current conditions.

Commission hearings commenced in Edmonton in February, 1935, and included visits to a number of Métis settlements. During its hearings, the commission also made it clear that it didn't intend any radical changes regarding Métis rights. And it also made clear that it didn't hold out a great deal of hope for Métis progress. For example, Judge Ewing agreed with a Catholic bishop, who asserted in his testimony that too much education was no good for the Métis. Health concerns received similarly short shrift. In response to concerns about deplorable health conditions, Judge Ewing replied that if things really were that bad he was sure the government would have sent out a doctor to the Métis communities.

The commission reported in February, 1936. The main recommendation was the establishment of a series of settlements for destitute Métis. Land would be set aside for them to farm and live on, with title to the land remaining in government hands. The commission stressed that "the plan could be launched with small expenditure". Its report should not be construed as meaning that the Métis had land rights — the scrip system established under the Dominion Lands Act had, according to the commission, extinguished "any supposed right which the half-breed had to special consideration." A settlement scheme would merely allow destitute Métis to escape their "actual condition of privation, penury and suffering". In its final report the commission stated that those Métis "who have settled down as farmers do not need nor...desire, public assistance. The term Half-Breed as used in this report has no application to such men."

Legislation giving the government authority to create Métis reserves was passed in 1938. The Métis Population Betterment Act defined Métis, and therefore all of those who would be permitted to live on reserves, as Métis who could not make an adequate living, that is, those who were destitute. In 1940 the Act was amended to provide that to be Métis one had to have at least one-quarter Indian blood. The first colony was established in 1939. Today, eight colonies are still in existence with a total population of 4,000. According to the Métis National Council the estimated total Métis population of Alberta is 60,000. The Alberta Métis who live outside the colonies find themselves in the same position as their brethren elsewhere.

Over the years problems cropped up with the colonies. In the summer of 1984 a joint government-Métis committee, chaired by author and former lieutenant-governor Grant MacEwan, reviewed the legislation and recommended that the Métis colonies be given the right to govern themselves. The committee also recommended the repeal of the Métis Betterment Act, transfer of title in the colonies to "settlement corporations" and that *Métis* be defined as "an individual of Aboriginal ancestry who identifies with Métis history and culture". In 1985 the Alberta government announced that it would be granting a measure of self-government to Alberta Métis, would be transferring title of colony lands to the Métis and would ensure that the colonies had some degree of constitutional protection.

The Saskatchewan government tried the Alberta approach to a limited degree. In 1940 six townships (a township is thirty-six square miles) of land were set aside at Green Lake (northwestern Saskatchewan) for the use of the Métis. The scheme was never given legislative sanction and no further colonies were established.

The Métis Situation Today

Over the decades since the 1940s, little progress has been made in resolving Métis grievances. They are still pressing for a resolution of their land claims and the right to govern their own affairs. Their situation is made even more difficult than that of other aboriginal people because of the constitutional debate as to whether they are under federal or provincial jurisdiction.

While the federal government has the responsibility under the Constitution for "Indians, and Lands reserved for the Indians" it has taken the view that Métis don't fall within that definition and are therefore a provincial responsibility. Quebec and Alberta, with the creation of the Métis colonies, are the only provinces to have taken clear responsibility for the Métis. Most other provinces have been quite content to leave the question of responsibility for the Métis in a legal limbo. Alternatively the federal government has taken the view that Métis land claims have been satisfied by the scrip system established under the Manitoba Act and the Dominion Lands Act. While both levels have denied responsibility for the Métis the federal government has, through various departments (Secretary of State, Department of Justice, Department of National Health and Welfare and other departments), established programs to assist Métis and non-status groups. Those programs include everything from funding Indian and Métis friendship centres, providing scholarships for Métis students to go to law school and giving grants for Métis and non-status Indians to participate in constitutional talks. Some scholars have argued that by establishing such programs Ottawa is in fact admitting constitutional responsibility for the Métis. To support this argument they point to historical facts wherein Ottawa made special provisions in the Manitoba Act and the Dominion Lands Act to settle Métis claims. Coupled with this is the fact that some Métis were included in some of the prairie treaties and on other occasions were given the choice of taking treaty or scrip. In fact, for many years the Indian Act, in defining *Indian*, specifically excluded people who had "received or...been allotted half-breed lands or money scrip". The counter-argument is that these programs are not aimed specifically at the Métis, but rather at an underprivileged group in society. Similarly, those who deny any special federal responsibility for the Métis point to the fact that many provinces have established special programs to assist the Métis people. Constitutional responsibility, of course, may mean an additional financial burden, therefore it is not surprising that each level of government seeks to place the burden on the other. (Prime Minister Brian Mulroney undertook during the 1985 constitutional conference on aboriginal rights to begin discussions with the Métis and non-status Indians regarding their claims, including land claims.)

If land is to be set aside for the Métis in the provinces, it will require the co-operation of both levels of government. Land resources and ownership rest with the provinces and it would be almost impossible for the federal government to establish a land base (except in the Yukon and the Northwest Territories) without provincial co-operation.

While governments have sidestepped the question of who is responsible for the Métis and have therefore avoided dealing with their grievances, the 1980s have been good years, representing a time of renewal for the Métis nation. The high point in their struggle for recognition has come with their mention in the Canadian Constitution. Canada's Constitution recognizes and affirms the existing treaty and aboriginal rights of Canada's aboriginal peoples. Aboriginal people are defined as including "the Indian, Inuit and Métis peoples of Canada". Presumably the reference to the Métis peoples means that the drafters of the Constitution (who included provincial premiers and attorney-generals along with federal cabinet ministers) recognized that the Métis have special rights that have to be protected. The Métis National Council, representing the Métis of western Canada, has taken the view that those rights include the right to a land base and the right to govern their own affairs.

The Constitution led to a series of constitutional conferences that attempted to define aboriginal rights more precisely. The first constitutional conference was held on March 15 and 16, 1983. The prime minister invited the Native Council of Canada to represent the Métis and non-status Indians. At a pre-conference ministerial meeting held on February 28, 1983, the Métis asked for and were denied a seat at the constitutional conference. The Métis then split from the Native Council of Canada and formed the Métis National Council. (The prairie Métis take the view they are a distinct people from non-status Indians and mixed-blood people in other provinces. Their claims are different, too, in that they primarily seek redress for historic grievances.) After commencing a court action in Ontario to obtain an injunction preventing the conference from proceeding without Métis representation, and after considerable lobbying, the Métis National Council succeeded in gaining an invitation to the constitutional conference.

In their declaration, prepared for the constitutional conference, the Métis stated:

> We, the Metis, are an historic aboriginal nation. During the 18th and 19th centuries, we developed our own cultural identity, lifestyle and political consciousness and asserted our rights through the formation of provisional governments in both Manitoba and Saskatchewan. Though defeated militarily at Batoche in 1885, we have waged an incessant struggle for justice through successive political associations.
>
> Today we again assert these, our inalienable aboriginal national rights, in our homeland in western Canada through the Metis National Council, the political voice of the Metis nationalist movement.
>
> The Métis National Council defines the Métis as: an aboriginal people distinct from Indians and Inuit; descendants of the historic Métis who evolved in what is now western Canada as a people with a common political will; descendants of those aboriginal peoples who have been absorbed by the historic Métis.

While the Métis have gained constitutional recognition there is still a long way to go before their grievances are dealt with.

The Métis in Manitoba are suing to get some of the land that they claim was promised under the Manitoba Act but never given to them. Other Métis in Manitoba have taken even further action. Almost a hundred years after the 1885 Rebellion, on April 16, 1984, the 350 Métis of Camperville, Manitoba (some 400 kilometres north of Winnipeg), declared themselves to be an independent nation, to get some action on their claims. They flew their own flag and declared absolute jurisdiction over education, justice, policing and over all wild game over some 200 square miles (approximately 500 square kilometres). This time the government sent no army; it simply ignored the Métis of Camperville. And that is the heart of the Métis complaint: the government has yet to take their grievances seriously.

7
The 1970s and 1980s: A Time of Change

The last three decades have been times of dramatic change for native rights in Canada. Native people have gone from having their demands ignored to playing an increasingly more noticeable role in Canada's political scene. The late sixties and early seventies were not happy times for native rights. In fact at that time the chance that native rights would gain any type of recognition and protection was rather slight.

In the 1960s the federal government was proceeding full steam ahead with its plan to assimilate Indians into the Canadian mainstream. In the mid-1960s the Department of Indian Affairs was offering Indian families $5,000 to relocate to the city. In 1967 the pot was sweetened even more. A $10,000 grant was offered to Indian families wishing to purchase a city home. A further $2,500 was available to assist with the purchase of furniture and appliances. This program was eventually discontinued.

Federal government intentions became abundantly clear on June 25, 1969, when the government announced its White Paper on Indian policy. The paper proposed: abolition of the Department of Indian Affairs and repeal of the Indian Act, transfer of all responsibility for Indian programs to the provinces, a policy to end treaties and a refusal to recognize aboriginal rights; in short, assimilation.

The government's dismissal of native demands forced many native people to look to demonstrations and militancy as ways of advancing their legitimate demands. Indian Affairs offices were occupied in Calgary and Ottawa. Bridges were blocked at Cornwall and near Montreal. A highway near Cache Creek, British Columbia, was blockaded to protest housing conditions.

There was a series of demonstrations in Kenora, Ontario. One of those resulted in a month-long armed occupation of Anicinabe Park by the Ojibway Warrior Society. The demonstrators demanded, amongst other things, return of the park to native people, improved human-rights legislation and better opportunities for native people.

In October 1974 the Native People's Caravan travelled from Vancouver to Ottawa to present their demands on the opening day of Parliament. Their most important demand was "the hereditary and treaty rights of all Native Peoples in Canada including Indian, Métis, Non-Status and Inuit must be recognized and respected in the constitution of Canada". Other demands included a repeal of the Indian Act and improved social conditions. The caravan never got to present its demands to Parliament. Barricades were erected and an RCMP tactical force, used for the first time on Parliament Hill, was eventually successful in driving the caravan off the Hill.

Less than a decade later (with the Trudeau Liberal government that had introduced the 1969 White Paper still in power) aboriginal and treaty rights were entrenched in the Constitution. Serious discussions were under way concerning the right of native people to govern themselves. By 1985, Thomas Berger, one of Canada's most prominent native rights advocates, was able to declare that Canada is "offering leadership in this area" and that the Alaska natives are looking "with envy on what has been achieved in Canada".

What had happened to create such a dramatic turn-about?

The Growth of Native Political Organizations

A great part of the turn-about can be attributed to the rapid growth of native organizations. Such organizations are a recent phenomenon. Historically, there have always been many impediments to their growth, including lack of funds and the active discouragement of the federal government. For many years a pass system existed in parts of western Canada making travel off the reserve difficult. Section 141 of the Indian Act (first introduced in 1927) made it an offence to raise funds for the purpose of advancing native claims.

Various organizational attempts were made in the early 1900s (even the 1800s). For the most part, the resulting organizations were limited in the people and area they represented. Often they were church-based, and folded after several years.

The 1930s and '40s saw the growth of provincial organizations. In 1931 the Tsimshian and Haida Indians founded the Native Brotherhood of British Columbia. After World War II, the North American Indian Brotherhood was formed in the interior of B.C. The Indian Association of Alberta was formed in 1939, the Union of Saskatchewan Indians (today called the Federation of Saskatchewan Indian Nations) in 1946. The CCF government in Saskatchewan encouraged, not always successfully, Indians and Métis to unite into provincial organizations.

The growth of native political organizations received two big boosts in the sixties: the first was the decision by the federal government (joined later by provincial governments) to provide funding for native organizations, and the second was the 1969 White Paper on Indian policy.

Federal government monies became available to native organizations in the mid-1960s. In 1963 the Centennial Commission provided $150,000 for projects by native organizations. In 1964, the secretary of state started to award the National Indian Council, formed in 1954, an annual grant for meetings. By 1970 federal funding from all departments to native organizations amounted to nearly $1 million.

At first the Department of Indian Affairs objected to the funding other departments were giving Indian organizations. However, it soon relented and began to provide provincial Indian organizations with one dollar per registered Indian. It also started funding the National Indian Brotherhood, formed in 1968 after the National Indian Council split into the NIB and the Canadian Métis Society. In 1969 the Privy Council granted $500,000 for native organizations to research claims and grievances.

The White Paper was the second factor that stimulated the growth of native political organizations. Faced with a proposal for the legal termination of their status, Indians began to organize. National and provincial Indian organizations suddenly gained a new life. They had gained a cause — their very existence as Indians.

Immediately after the release of the White Paper, Indian spokesmen started to make the news in voicing opposition to it. Position papers and books by Indian authors began to appear, the most famous being *The Unjust Society, The Tragedy of Canada's Indians* by

Harold Cardinal. Published in 1969, the book summarized native demands and complaints.

Not only did the White Paper stimulate Indian organization, but it showed Indian organizations that they could achieve success through lobbying, organizing and protesting. In June 1970, the federal government announced that it would not be proceeding with the White Paper. In Trudeau's words to Indian leaders, "…we won't force any solution on you, because we are not looking for any particular solution."

The growth in native political power in the sixties can be documented in numbers alone. In the 1950s there was one national native organization and nine provincial ones. By the sixties there were four national, one regional and thirty-three provincial organizations.

The Political Climate

Coupled with the growth in native organizations was the parallel growth in support groups. The most active was the Indian-Eskimo Association (later re-named the Canadian Association in Support of the Native People) formed in 1957 to act as a lobbying force on behalf of native people.

Another important factor in bringing native issues to public attention was the Hawthorn Report. In early 1963 Harry Hawthorn was asked by the federal government to survey Indian conditions; he organized a team of fifty-two social scientists. They produced their first report, "A Survey of the Contemporary Indians of Canada," in 1966. The report concluded that Indians suffered from poverty, underemployment and various other social problems. The report also concluded that Indians should have full rights as citizens of Canada and the provinces in which they lived, plus the special privileges associated with their status. In short, "citizens plus".

Various Canadian authors were also bringing native issues to public attention. One was Heather Robertson in her 1970 book, *Reservations are for Indians*.

The Red Power movement was having an impact. More than one Canadian, looking at the racial riots in the United States, feared that the same thing would happen in Canada. The armed occupation of Anicinabe Park in Kenora, Ontario, and the near riot on Parliament Hill made it clear to Canadians that Canada was not immune to racial tensions.

The threat of racial violence probably made some Canadians realize that compromise was necessary on native rights issues. It was the fear of escalating violence that led the government to create, in 1975, a joint Cabinet-National Indian Brotherhood committee to "establish a process designed to yield agreements between government and representatives of Indian people on major policy issues". The committee came to an end in 1978 when the NIB pulled out. Reason: the government saw the committee as an advisory body, the NIB saw it as a negotiating forum.

Just as the federal consultative process broke down at the national level, it started to flourish in Ontario; 1978 saw the establishment of the Indian Commission of Ontario, a tripartite council made up of the federal and provincial governments and the Indian Chiefs of Ontario, for the purpose of negotiating and dealing with issues of mutual concern.

Native rights received a further boost with the January 1973 Supreme Court of Canada decision in *Calder* v. *The Attorney-General of British Columbia*. The Nishga sued for a declaration that they had aboriginal title. Their case failed on procedural grounds; however, six of the seven judges hearing the case recognized that aboriginal rights existed, and three of those six said that the Nishgas still had aboriginal rights.

Prior to this decision the government had denied the existence of aboriginal rights. Shortly after this decision in August 1973, the government announced a comprehensive land claims policy that recognized two broad categories of claims; comprehensive claims based on aboriginal rights and specific claims based on specific legal commitments. Funding was made available for researching native claims and in 1974 an Office of Native Claims was created to review claims. During the same time native groups began asserting their claims and setting forth their positions. In 1975 the Dene Nation (Indians and Métis in the Western NWT) in their Manifesto became one of the first aboriginal groups to assert nationhood within Canada. The next year the Inuit Tapirisat proposed a land claims settlement which included an Inuit-governed territory known as Nunavut (our land). By 1978 the National Indian Brotherhood had identified constitutional reform as a major priority of Indian people.

Native Rights in the Constitution

The greatest boost to the recognition of native rights came with Canada's new Constitution and more particularly the negotiation process leading up to it. The constitutional process proved that Indian leaders and organizations could influence the national agenda.

Discussion about constitutional patriation and reform originated with the 1927 Dominion-Provincial Conference, but it was not until the mid-1970s that the process began in earnest, sparked by Quebec nationalism, western alienation and Pierre Trudeau's personal interest in constitutional reform.

By 1978, the federal government was ready to move and native rights was on the agenda. Its White Paper on constitutional reform stated that recognition of aboriginal rights was one of the principles to guide the renewal of Confederation. Later in the year, the federal government introduced Bill C-60 to amend the Constitution. The bill contained some limited protection for native rights — native rights based on the Royal Proclamation of 1763 were to be immune from being overridden by the bill's proposed Charter of Rights.

In response the NIB made two demands: first, that aboriginal and treaty rights be entrenched in the Constitution and second, that native people be involved in the constitutional process. At the October 1978 First Ministers' Conference on the Constitution, the NIB along with the Native Council of Canada and the Inuit Tapirisat of Canada were granted observer status. At the next first ministers' meeting, in February 1979, the ministers agreed that constitutional discussions would include ''Canada's Native People and the Constitution''. The NIB objected to having only observer status, their general assembly passed a resolution asking the Queen to halt patriation until aboriginal rights were fully recognized and armed with this resolution, they began lobbying in the United Kingdom to block patriation.

Constitutional discussions continued throughout 1979 and 1980. In September 1980, when there had still been no progress, Trudeau announced that the federal government would proceed unilaterally with patriation.

While all this was going on, native people were gaining support from various sources for constitutional protection of their rights. Support came from Parliamentarians, lawyers and church groups.

A Joint Senate-House of Commons committee concluded:

> In many respects the native peoples of Canada are a test of Canadian society: a test of its compassion to reach out for new and deeper values of tolerance and friendship; a test of its laws to do justice to the weak and the few; a test of its willingness to share the nation's wealth, and to give equality of opportunity a chance, freedom a new birth, and self-respect a new home in the minds and hearts of Canada's native peoples.

Support also came from the Task Force on Canadian Unity, jointly chaired by John Robarts and Jean-Luc Pépin. In their 1979 report they stated:

> Both central and provincial authorities should pursue direct discussions with representatives of Canadian Indians, Inuit and Métis, with a view to arriving at mutually acceptable constitutional provisions that would secure the rightful place of native peoples in Canadian society.

At its August 1980 annual meeting, the Canadian Bar Association (the national lawyers' group) passed the following resolution:

> That there be special constitutional provisions for native peoples incorporated in any revision of the Constitution of Canada...

Church leaders, such as the Primate of the Anglican Church in Canada, the Most Reverend Edward Scott, and the Ontario Conference of Catholic Bishops also spoke out for constitutional protection of native rights; and other support groups expressed their solidarity.

Such public support did not have much effect on the federal government. After deciding in the fall of 1980 to proceed unilaterally, the Trudeau government introduced another constitutional bill. There was no constitutional guarantee of native rights.

Pierre Trudeau explained the government's position when he spoke in Parliament on November 7, 1980.

> I think the simple claim of aboriginal rights, without knowing exactly what it means, is not a matter which one can convincingly argue should be put in the Constitution at this time. First of all, the courts would be called upon to interpret such a constitutional amendment, and I think everyone would want to know what aboriginal rights are, what [is] their extent, to whom they apply, and so on.

Native people stepped up their lobbying in both London, England and in Ottawa. The most publicized was the "constitutional express" of November 1980. Starting in Vancouver the train brought over 1,000 Indian people to Ottawa to lobby MPs. At the same time native leaders were meeting in London with the Foreign Affairs Committee; others were lobbying the United Nations.

The lobbying proved to be effective. On January 30, 1981, then federal Justice Minister Jean Chrétien introduced an amendment to the proposed constitution guaranteeing aboriginal rights. That amendment provided:

> The aboriginal and treaty rights of the aboriginal peoples of Canada are hereby recognized and affirmed.
> In this Act, "aboriginal peoples of Canada" includes the Indian, Inuit and Métis peoples of Canada.

The provisions that ensured that the Charter of Rights would not override native rights was strengthened. The act also mentioned that a constitutional conference would be held within two years of the Constitution's becoming law, for the purpose of defining aboriginal rights. Aboriginal representatives would be invited to the conference.

The changes received mixed response. The NIB wanted a clause inserted that the constitutional provisions affecting aboriginal people could only be changed with their consent. They also sought constitutional recognition for the right to self-government. Lobbying in London continued. A group of Alberta Indian chiefs petitioned the Queen and the British government to refrain from patriating the Constitution until all Indian claims were satisfied. They also started a court action for a declaration that treaty Indians were the responsibility of England because treaties had been signed with the Queen.

The proposed federal Constitution (after pressure and opposition from the provinces) was referred to the Supreme Court of Canada to determine whether the federal government could unilaterally repatriate the constitution. In a seven-to-two judgement the Supreme Court ruled in Ottawa's favour, but six judges went on to say that the usual practice was that constitutional amendments should have a substantial measure of support from the provinces.

Ottawa and the provinces sat down at the bargaining table and came up with an agreement on November 5, 1981. Aboriginal people did not participate at this meeting. The agreed-upon Constitution did, however, have a significant impact upon native people. The section guaranteeing treaty and aboriginal rights was dropped. The requirement for a constitutional conference remained. So did the section which protected native rights from the Charter of Rights.

Why were the constitutional guarantees dropped? According to Jean Chrétien in his book *Straight From the Heart*, "To get the consent of the majority of the provinces, the federal government had to settle for an incomplete guarantee of rights for women and to drop aboriginal rights from the charter."

The reaction from the native community was swift. "Native leaders shocked," read the *Globe and Mail* headline of November 6. Chief George Manuel of the Union of British Columbia Indians said that all Indian rights were threatened and saw this as a move to assimilate Indians. Inuit children in Arctic Bay, NWT, were kept out of school for two weeks in protest.

Adverse reaction came from many non-native sources as well. Liberal Senator and Minister of State Jack Austin stated that he was disappointed that the native rights clause was chopped from the Constitution. British Columbia Supreme Court Judge Thomas Berger voiced his opposition, and said, "I never would have believed that this would happen." Berger's comments eventually ended up costing him his judgeship.

Strong reaction from native leaders and the public brought about a quick change. By mid-November the provinces began to change their positions. The Conservative government in Manitoba had been defeated and the new NDP government quickly announced that it would support constitutional recognition of native rights. Premier Blakeney of Saskatchewan and Davis of Ontario also announced support for the entrenchment of native rights in the Constitution. The last holdout was Alberta Premier Lougheed. He suggested that the word *existing* be included. His suggestion was accepted and the proposed change read:

> The existing aboriginal and treaty rights of the aboriginal peoples of Canada are hereby recognized and affirmed.

A year and a half later, at the 1983 constitutional conference Lougheed explained his reasons for insisting on the change.

> The proposed aboriginal rights provision was open to the interpretation, however, that it would create new aboriginal rights that were not previously recognized in law...In effect, it [the addition of "existing"] was a commitment by governments to protect the aboriginal rights which exist now and to recognize those which may come into existence as a result of this conference.

In early December, the new Constitution cleared Parliament. It recognized and affirmed existing treaty and aboriginal rights, and defined aboriginal people as being the Indian, Inuit and Métis people. It also required that there be a constitutional conference, to which aboriginal people would be invited, to discuss the identification and definition of aboriginal rights. Finally, that proposed bill stated that the Charter of Rights would not take away the rights of Indian people arising from any land claims settlement or from the Royal Proclamation of 1763. Aboriginal rights are group rights, and it was therefore necessary to have a section that protected those rights against the individual-rights sections of the Charter.

The constitution was off to London for approval, but Canada's native people were not entirely happy. They had two main concerns: the insertion of the word "existing," and their belief, which had not been taken into consideration, that the Constitution should require native consent to any amendment affecting native rights. The ease with which their rights had been deleted in the proposed Constitution was very fresh in their minds. Delegations of native people left for London to lobby the British Parliament and commence court action to block patriation. In the end neither approach proved to be successful but they did gain some public support. Canada's Constitution eventually cleared the English Parliament without any great hurdles.

In spite of its limitations it does provide protection for aboriginal people that did not exist before. It ensures that aboriginal rights cannot be taken away unilaterally or without the consent of aboriginal people. In British Columbia several judges (including three judges of the Supreme Court of Canada in the Nishgas' case), lawyers and politicians have argued that early colonial legislation had the effect of extinguishing aboriginal rights. Today, because of constitutional protection for aboriginal rights a government could no longer unilaterally legislate aboriginal rights out of existence. Unfortunately, the Constitution does not restore those rights that may have been taken away prior to its enactment. Thus, assuming no agreement, it is still necessary to have a court determine whether aboriginal rights survived the British Columbia colonial legislation that opened up the land for settlement.

The Constitution also ensures that neither federal nor provincial legislation can take away treaty rights. Thus, today federal legislation such as the Migratory Birds Convention Act would be found to be non-applicable to treaty Indians who had received a guarantee of hunting and fishing rights. Again, however, the Constitution does not restore rights that were taken away before the Constitution was proclaimed. In several decisions the courts have said that only those rights in existence on April 17, 1982, are constitutionally protected.

The Constitutional Conferences

With pomp and ceremony Canada's new Constitution came into force on April 17, 1982. That, however, was merely the beginning of the struggle for greater constitutional recognition of native rights. The Constitution guaranteed a constitutional conference within one year to identify and define aboriginal rights.

The conference was held on March 15 and 16, 1983. Not all native organizations agreed to participate. Some native communities (a minority) took the position that they are sovereign nations, and that to participate in the constitutional process would be an admission that they are subject to Canadian jurisdiction. These groups have taken this stand out of a genuine fear of cultural and political assimilation.

Considerable progress was made at the 1983 conference, compared with later conferences. First, there was agreement that no constitutional changes would be made affecting aboriginal rights without a constitutional conference to which aboriginal people would be invited. (This did not go as far as some Indian leaders had hoped — that is, an absolute veto over constitutional change affecting them). The parties agreed that another constitutional conference would be held in 1984, agreed on the agenda for that meeting, and further agreed that in addition to the 1984 conference two other conferences would be held before 1987. The constitutional guarantee for existing treaty and aboriginal rights was extended to include future land claims agreements. Finally, the Constitution was amended to guarantee sexual equality in aboriginal rights. While there was agreement in principle on aboriginal rights applying equally to men and women, immediately after the conference the Inuit organization and the Native Council of Canada declared that the wording had been changed without their consent. This change, or alleged change (government parties denied there had been a change in wording), led to considerable acrimony at future conferences. A great deal of energy was spent at the 1984 and 1985 constitutional conferences trying to come up with a better equality section.

Besides the sexual equality issue, a great deal of the discussion at the 1984 and 1985 conferences was devoted to self-government. While both Trudeau in 1984 and Mulroney in 1985 pressed for some constitutional recognition of the right to self-government, both were unsuccessful, either because of provincial objections or because native organizations rejected proposals as being too watered down. The 1984 federal proposal read in part:

> The government of Canada and the provincial governments are committed to negotiating with representatives of the aboriginal peoples of Canada to identify the nature, jurisdiction and powers of self-governing institutions that will meet the needs of their communities...

The federal proposal suggested that the Constitution be amended to provide that "the aboriginal peoples of Canada have the right to self-governing institutions" with the actual power of those institutions being a matter of negotiation. Ontario, Manitoba and New Brunswick supported the federal proposal; other provinces, including B.C., Alberta and Saskatchewan, strongly opposed it.

Aboriginal leaders also had concerns. Their fear was that there was nothing in the federal proposal to constitutionally entrench the self-governing institutions that were negotiated. The native people wanted not only the principle but the actual institutions protected by the Constitution.

In 1985, Brian Mulroney came to the constitutional conference with a similar proposal. He proposed that the general principle of self-government be recognized in the Constitution along with a commitment by the federal and provincial governments to negotiate the establishment of native governments on a regional basis. In Mulroney's words:

> Let us decide at this conference that our constitution shall acknowledge that aboriginal peoples have a right to self-government. Let us agree that we will work out together, over time and on a case-by-case basis, the different means, constitutional and otherwise, that will be required to respond to the special circumstances of different aboriginal communities.

But they could not agree, and despite there being more support from both the provinces and the native organizations, there was still a big gap between some of the provinces and the native organizations.

The chief objection from the provinces was that Indian self-government had not been defined. They wanted it spelled out in detail before they agreed to any constitutional entrenchment.

Native people's greatest fear has been that only general principles will be enshrined in the Constitution, and that the actual native government institutions that will be established will not be protected by the Constitution. Native leaders feel that, too often, governments have unilaterally taken away or changed their rights and that the only protection against such unilateral action is a constitutional guarantee. Some native leaders objected to the 1985 Mulroney proposal because it only committed governments to begin negotiations but not to complete them.

The Constitution requires that another constitutional conference on aboriginal rights be held before April 17, 1987. There has also been discussion about continuing the process of constitutional talks beyond 1987.

In spite of the limited progress made at the constitutional conferences, the process should not be regarded as a failure. The conferences mark a major departure from earlier national policy. This was the first time that native peoples were actively consulted (and on national television) regarding their rights. It was the first time that native leaders have been able to address all of Canada's political leaders in a national forum. The widespread coverage that the conferences received (to date they have all been televised) has meant that more people have become aware of native issues. They have become issues of national concern to a great majority of Canadians. The constitutional conferences have also meant a boost in morale for the native community — seeing their leaders meeting on an equal basis with Canada's national leaders has given them a far greater confidence that there is a place for them in Canada.

Parliamentary Committee on Self-Government

There have been other developments that have advanced native issues, among them the work of the Special Parliamentary Committee on Indian Self-Government in Canada. In 1982 the Standing Committee on Indian

Affairs and Northern Development asked the House of Commons for authority to examine "the Government of Canada's total financial and other relationships" with Indian people. In response to that request the Commons appointed the special committee. Sixty public meetings were held across Canada, at which 567 witnesses spoke. A representative of the Assembly of First Nations participated as an ex-officio member and the Native Women's Association of Canada and the Native Council of Canada were represented by liaison members. The all-party committee, chaired by Liberal MP Keith Penner, reported in November 1983. Their report was unanimous.

It recommended that the federal government recognize native people's right to self-government and that such a right be entrenched in the Constitution. The committee recommended that the existing land base for Indian people be expanded, that land claims be settled and that control of all resources on Indian lands be turned over to Indian people. These latter recommendations were made to ensure that Indian governments had an adequate economic base to guarantee financial viability. The committee recommended that Indian governments should have the power to legislate in areas such as social and cultural affairs, education, family relations, land and resource use, revenue raising, economic and commercial development, justice and law enforcement. (In short, something close to the powers provinces have). The report envisaged that there might be regional Indian governments to ensure maximum efficiency of resources. Abolition of the Department of Indian Affairs was another key recommendation. In its place the committee envisaged a Ministry of State for Indian First Nations Relations. An independent office would be established to monitor and report to Parliament on official actions affecting Indian First Nations. Similarly there would be an advocacy office, controlled by Indian nations, to represent Indian nations in legal disputes. To put Indian self-government into place the committee recommended an independent secretariat, jointly appointed by the federal government and Indian organizations, to provide a neutral forum for conducting negotiations.

The committee report received quick response from the then Liberal government. On June 27, 1984 the government introduced its Indian Self-Government Bill, but it died with the defeat of the government.

International Recognition of Aboriginal Rights

Equally significant is the fact that since the Second World War there has been a growing concern by the international community about the plight of indigenous people. The term "indigenous" is used internationally with a meaning similar to "aboriginal", that is, denoting people existing in a land at the dawn of history, before the arrival of colonists. Besides the Americas, there are indigenous peoples in Japan, Scandinavia, the Philippines, the Soviet Union and in parts of Asia. In Canada, the Métis, being the product of contact between colonists and indigenous people, might strictly speaking not fall within the international definition.

The Special Parliamentary Committee on Indian Self-Government recognized the importance of the international forum. The committee concluded:

> Canada is obliged to protect and promote the rights of the peoples of the Indian First Nations in a manner consistent with the rights guaranteed in the international covenants Canada has signed — The United Nations Covenant on Economic, Social and Cultural

Rights, the Covenant on Civil and Political Rights, and the Helsinki Final Act of 1975.

Canada's native people have also recognized the importance of the international forum for advancing their rights. They have lobbied at the United Nations and have argued their cause before other international institutions. Indigenous people from other countries have also looked to the international community for recognition of their rights. One of the things indigenous people are pressing for is an agreement establishing international guarantees of their rights in all countries where they live.

The first mention of indigenous people in international agreements was in Convention 107 of the International Labour Organisation. Adopted in 1957, the convention requires countries to give equal protection to Indians in their national laws and it prohibits discrimination against Indians in employment, health care and education. The convention also recognizes the rights of tribes to occupy their traditional lands. The convention is not regarded by native people as an important document, as the theme of the agreement is to facilitate the ''progressive integration'' of indigenous populations into ''their respective national communities''. In short, assimilation, something that is rejected by most native people in Canada and abroad. Canada, incidentally, did not sign this agreement. The ILO is currently in the process of trying to come up with a new convention on indigenous people.

More important to native people has been the International Covenant on Civil and Political Rights, which amongst other things guarantees that ''all peoples have the right of self-determination''. And it was under this agreement that Sandra Lovelace took her case against

Canada to the United Nations. Lovelace complained that Canada had contravened Article 27 of the covenant, which provides that:

> In those States in which ethnic, religious or linguistic minorities exist, persons belonging to such minorities shall not be denied the right, in community with the other members of their group, to enjoy their own culture, to profess and practise their own religion, or to use their own religion, or to use their own language.

Lovelace was a Maliseet Indian but lost her status by marriage to a non-Indian in 1970. Therefore, she was no longer entitled to live on her reserve and she argued that she was therefore hindered in practising her culture and language. The United Nations Human Rights Committee found that while legally she was not an Indian, ethnically she was, and therefore she was denied her rights under Article 27 because the reserve was the only place where she could fully exercise those rights.

The committee could not, of course, legally force Canada to change its law when it reached its decision in 1981. However, internationally Canada has long been an advocate of human rights; to be cited as having breached the International Covenant on Civil and Political Rights was an embarrassment.

Other UN agencies have also been looking at the issue of indigenous rights. Immediately following the creation of the United Nations, the Human Rights Commission (a separate body from that which heard the Lovelace case) organized a Sub-Commission on the Prevention of Discrimination and Protection of Minorities. Early in its work, the sub-commission undertook a separate study of the discrimination indigenous people face. The massive study, which took a decade to complete, details the conditions of indigenous people around the world. While the report has been the subject of some controversy it does contain a number of progressive ideas, including the recommendation that indigenous people should have a degree of autonomy in their own affairs.

At the same time, the Economic and Social Council of the United Nations (the parent body of the Human Rights Commission) asked the sub-commission to set up a Special Working Group on Indigenous Populations. Formed in 1982, the working group's mandate is: 1) to review developments pertaining to the promotion and protection of the human rights and fundamental freedoms of indigenous populations and 2) to give special attention to the evolution of standards concerning rights of indigenous populations. While the work of the group is in some jeopardy because of the United Nations' financial situation, the hope of indigenous peoples is that the group's work will eventually lead to an international agreement on the treatment of indigenous people. Canada's native groups have been particularly active in presenting information and evidence to the working group.

There is an equal amount of international activity at the unofficial level. The United Nations Charter specifically makes provision for non-governmental agencies to be involved in UN work. A number of these are specifically concerned with indigenous rights. they include: Four Directions Council (c/o Innu Kanantuapatshet Sheshatshit, Labrador); Indian Council of South America, Lima, Peru; Indian Law Resource Center, Washington; International Indian Treaty Council, New York; Inuit Circumpolar Conference, Anchorage; National Indian Youth Council, Albuquerque; Survival International, Washington and London; and World Council of Indigenous Peoples, Ottawa. In 1977 the UN NGOs held a conference in Geneva on discrimination against indigenous populations, which produced a draft Declaration of Principles for the Defence of the Indigenous Nations and Peoples of the Western Hemisphere.

Not all international activity has centred around the United Nations. The Fourth Russell Tribunal (sponsored by the Bertrand Russell Peace Foundation), held in Rotterdam in 1980, dealt specifically with the rights of Indians in the Americas. Twelve complaints were heard by the tribunal, including two from Canada. The tribunal jury found that Canada had failed to involve its aboriginal people in the constitutional amendment process.

International support groups have sprung up to assist indigenous peoples. Examples of two such groups are Survival International (based in London and Washington) and International Work Group for Indigenous Affairs, in Copenhagen. The work of most of these support groups is twofold: first, to bring to the world's attention the deplorable conditions of some indigenous peoples' lives; and second, to develop international guarantees for indigenous peoples' rights.

Do these international activities make any difference? A cynical Canadian might ask: who cares what the UN says or what some unofficial body like Survival International thinks? International activities do make a difference. International pressure can influence domestic policy, especially in a country like Canada, which prides itself on being a champion of international human rights. And activists point out that international lobbying played an important role in the abolition of slavery.

Native groups and their supporters are hoping that their efforts will help make the recognition of indigenous rights an international issue on the scale of apartheid in South Africa.

Much remains to be done to make indigenous rights an international issue. While the situation of Canada's indigenous peoples leaves plenty of room for improvement, the situation in other parts of the world is far worse. In Central and South America, indigenous people have gained almost no recognition for their rights. In fact, in many of those countries, they face not only appalling poverty, but physical dispossession and in some cases even the threat of extinction (sometimes by disease and sometimes by machine-gun). Most Central and South American nations have large Indian populations. Canada, the US, New Zealand, Finland and Norway have probably made the greatest progress in protecting their indigenous populations. Some progress in recognizing aboriginal rights has been made in Australia. Finland has taken a number of steps to recognize the rights of its Sami population, including the establishment of a Sami Parliament. The Soviet Union has allegedly started a number of economic self-sufficiency programs to help its indigenous populations (including such things as a reindeer industry, manned by indigenous people) but has been reluctant to recognize separate rights for them. However, there is a scarcity of information in the West about what is happening in the USSR. In all countries with aboriginal people, much remains to be done to see that their rights are protected.

Indigenous groups are hoping that international pressure will force countries with aboriginal populations to ensure their cultural survival and the recognition of their right to have their own land. Some of the credit for putting indigenous rights on the world stage has to go to Canadian native groups.

8
The Future of Native Rights

Fifteen years hence, as one drives down the road, the sign might read:

> WELCOME TO THE NATION OF OUR LAND.
> You are now entering the Our Land Indian Reserve
> governed by the Our Land Nation. You are subject to
> the laws and jurisdiction of the Our Land Nation. The
> Our Land Nation is a part of the Wapati Regional
> Indian Government.

Driving into the reserve, one sees Ms. Lonehunter working in her garden. She has just sent her children, Michael and Sarah, to the Our Land Primary School, run by the Wapati Indian School Board (which operates as an independent commission of the Wapati government). Ms. Lonehunter waves to Constable Squirrel, who drives by in a police car bearing the words "Wapati Police, a division of the Wapati Regional Indian Government". Ms. Lonehunter is hoping that today's band council meeting will approve the extension of water and sewer services to her house. (Purely local matters, such as water and sewer hook-ups, are handled at the reserve level by the reserve council rather than by the regional government).

Our Land is an Indian Reserve of 400 square kilometres; it has a population of 1,200 band members. The nation's Constitution states that everyone who is a descendant of the Our Land tribe and is accepted by the community is a citizen (there are rules whereby any member of the community can complain to a tribal judge about someone else's status as an Our Lander, and the judge will hear both sides and decide).

Several years ago the Our Land nation started its own school. Because the reserve's resources are limited, the reserve found it difficult to run an education system. Eventually it joined the Wapati Indian School Board, which now has jurisdiction over the school. The board developed the curriculum, hired the teachers and oversees the general operation of the school. Children are taught in both the native language and English. The teachers are tribal members who took teacher education at university but have now returned. Tribal elders often visit the school to talk about traditions and religious practices.

The Our Landers have also given up jurisdiction to the Wapati Regional Indian Government in other areas besides education, including policing and justice services, economic development policies, and cultural and social welfare matters. The Wapati Government is made up of four neighbouring reserves. Amongst other services the Wapati Government has established a medical service on the Our Land Reserve. In fact, there are clinics on each reserve, staffed on a part-time basis. The health team spends one day a week on each reserve. The cost of the health service, like all the other costs associated with the Wapati Government, is shared by the four reserves. The four reserves also share a police service. Under a contractual arrangement the police can call on the RCMP should additional help be needed. The police enforce the Criminal Code of Canada as well as traffic, liquor and other laws made by the band council on each reserve. The laws are published and are available in each band office. They are also distributed in the schools. The police spend a lot of time mediating disputes and only charge people as a last resort. A judge appointed by the Wapati Government travels to each reserve once a week to hear cases. He is from one of the reserves making up the Wapati Government.

Revenues to run the government are raised from selling business licences and from oil royalties. The federal government also makes an annual grant.

This fictional scenario might well be reality in Canada in another decade, as native self-government comes closer to fruition. Native self-government is the issue of the 1980s and will probably continue to be an important issue in Canadian politics, well into the 1990s. The self-government debate provides a unique opportunity for the Canadian government to redefine its relationship with native people. In doing so, Canada may well reshape the nature of the federal structure. Federalism has been redefined to accommodate other pressures (such as the needs and aspirations of Quebec, and the needs of francophone citizens outside Quebec) and there is no reason why the federal structure should not be reshaped to accommodate the aspirations of Canada's native peoples.

Reasons for Self-Government

There are two bases on which native people advance their claim for self-government. First, a natural desire on the part of people to run their own affairs. It was such a desire which fuelled the decolonization drive in much of the Third World. It is this desire that has brought Blacks in South Africa into violent confrontation with the South African government.

As a signatory to the International Covenant on Civil and Political Rights, Canada has internationally recognized the desire for self-determination. The covenant states:

> All peoples have the right of self-determination. By virtue of that right they freely determine their political status and freely pursue their economic, social and cultural development.

The Helsinki Accords of 1975, to which Canada was a party, reaffirmed the right to self-determination.

Self-determination does not necessarily mean independence. It means however, that a people (like the indigenous peoples of the world) should have a say about the terms and conditions under which they are incorporated into a nation. In other words incorporation into a state should be a people's voluntary decision, not one forced upon them.

Canada's aboriginal people argue not only that they have the right to self-determination, but that they have had this right since time immemorial. They point out that they governed themselves before the arrival of the Europeans and have never given up their right to do so.

The second ground on which native people claim self-government is that, to date, Canadian policies regarding them have been disastrous and that the only remedy is self-government.

In negotiating self-government, and changes to Indian government institutions as they are developed, Canada needs to look carefully at its past policies so that past mistakes can be avoided. It would be futile to develop native government institutions that would have to function under the shadow of past policies.

Past Native Policies and Self-Government

Canada's native policy so far can be characterized by a number of constants. First, there has been considerable confusion and contradiction in Indian policy. On the one hand there has been a concerted effort to assimilate the native population into the Canadian mainstream. This has been evidenced by policies such as the outlawing Indian cultural beliefs, and legislative provisions whereby Indians could renounce their status (called enfranchisement). Government efforts to assimilate Indians were supported by other factions of society — such as schoolteachers who forbade the use of native languages in schools, and priests who tried to Christianize the Indians. On the other hand, policymakers saw Indians as being "like children and unable to make their own way". Hence the policies of segregating Indians on reserves, and the passing of special laws for Indians, including laws regarding liquor consumption and Indian will-making power. It is hard to assimilate people if you segregate them and treat them differently.

Slowly, Canada is working its way out of that conundrum thanks to the fact that Canadians are beginning to see their country as a multicultural society (multiculturalism is now constitutionally enshrined) and are rejecting the notion of assimilation.

Another constant in Canadian policy has been the failure to consult native people in a meaningful way on matters affecting them. No better example illustrates this point than the preparation of the 1969 White Paper. Consultations with native leaders were being held, while at the same time senior government officials were secretly working on a policy to abolish Indian status. The constitutional conferences represent a first step in a policy change that may see more active and meaningful consultation with the Indian population.

The debate over the division of responsibility for native people between federal and provincial governments has been yet another constant in Canadian policy. Since Confederation, each level of government has tried to shift more of their responsibilities unto the other.

In the 1930s Ottawa and Quebec went to the Supreme Court of Canada to decide who was responsible for the Inuit in Quebec. Similarly, there has been an ongoing debate over who is responsible for the Métis.

In a major revision of the Indian Act in 1951 the federal government introduced a change (without consulting the Indians, of course) whereby provincial laws of general application would apply to Indian people unless they contradicted the Indian Act or any treaty made with the Indians. This change was seen by many legal scholars as Ottawa's attempt to make more provincial standards applicable to Indians and make Indian reserves into something akin to municipalities.

This was followed by the 1969 White Paper, which stated: ''Propose to the governments of the provinces that they take over the same responsibility for Indians that they have for other citizens in their provinces''. Only two provinces, Ontario and Saskatchewan, supported the White Paper.

Seventeen years later, in 1986, a task force reviewing federal government expenditures, under the stewardship of Deputy Prime Minister Erik Nielsen, recommended cuts in Indian programming. Such cuts, the review said, could be achieved by transferring some of the responsibility for Indians to the provinces.

In short, such constitutional squabbles, the assimilate-or-segregate contradictions and the consistent lack of consultation with native peoples have led to policies that have hindered and set native people back rather than helping them.

What is Self-Government?

No issue of native rights has provoked as much debate, concern and fear in the non-native community as the issue of self-government. For many Canadians, self-government means independent nations — they see little countries spread across the Canadian map, each issuing its own passports, having its own embassies, and so on.

There is no one definition of self-government. It is an evolving process and ideas advocated today may no longer be advanced ten years from now. And when native government institutions are developed, time will show what works and what does not. At the present time it is impossible to define precisely the model that native governments will follow. Differing forms of government will be required for different areas of Canada. The type of governmental structures that will work for the Inuit of the north might be entirely inappropriate for the Indians of Walpole Island (in southwestern Ontario). The revenue base that will be available to native governments will also greatly influence the form of the government. In spite of the fact that it is impossible to describe a model for Indian self-government, there are certain things that can be said about it.

First, a caveat needs to be sounded. There is the danger that governments may be tempted to dictate the form native self-government should take. An equal danger is consultants defining what self-government means. If any lesson is clear from history it is that native people must be given the opportunity to define their own structures.

As a starting point, self-government means native people having a greater say about the terms under which they are incorporated into the federal system. The self-government debate should be seen as federalism growing (Canada's federal structure should not be seen as a static institution) and as a process whereby the terms of native entry into Confederation are being worked out. The Quebec-Ottawa relationship is an example of how Confederation can evolve to meet needs.

There are three basic models of native self-government. The first means a sovereign state, completely independent of Canada. With the exception of a very small minority most native people have rejected this model. What native people are asking for is a fairer deal in Canada, not independence.

At the other end of the spectrum would be native communities having a status similar to municipalities. This model has been generally rejected by most native leaders. They see municipal government structures as being too limited to meet native aspirations. First, municipal governments are under the control of a superior government (in Canada municipalities, be they large cities or villages, are created by provincial statute and must operate within rules set by the province). Indian leaders feel that such a structure would offer them very little guarantee for the future — if they are subject to the whims of a senior government their whole government could be taken away at some future time. Moreover, native leaders want their governments to have power over things like education (including the language of instruction and the content taught), cultural affairs and justice (the rules by which the society operates.) Currently, all of those subjects are beyond the jurisdiction of municipal governments in Canada (though, in fairness, large municipalities have some influence in the area of cultural policy and law enforcement). Similarly, native communities want to determine economic and industrial policy — again, an area in which municipalities have limited authority.

The third model involves something in between independent nationhood and municipal status. The model would be something close to provincehood, in which native governments would in certain areas (banking, monetary system, postal system, foreign affairs, transportation, etc.) be subject to the federal government, but would have autonomy in other areas such as education, economic policies, justice policies (including a police force, a court system and the power to make their own laws), health care, cultural policy and other areas. Such a native government would have authority to tax (as do provinces), and would have full control over lands within the jurisdiction of the government. Such a government might also involve some jurisdiction over criminal law and divorce. Currently, provinces have no jurisdiction in those areas. While this is a model to which many native people aspire, many Canadians, including many political leaders, are hesitant to create governments with such extensive powers.

Justice is one area that illustrates why native governments need something more than a municipal type of government. It is also an area in which considerable work has been done in developing workable models for native governments. There are several research projects under way within native organizations developing native justice systems.

Indian and Inuit leaders point out that many laws in Canada are inconsistent with native culture and traditions. They point to such areas as dispute resolution, deciding what is a wrong against the whole community (under the Canadian system wrongs against the community are called crimes and the system of law for dealing with such is known as criminal law), how wrongs against the community should be dealt with, family matters and matters involving children. They point out, for example, that in traditional native societies the emphasis was on mediation, not punishment, and that concepts of property were that property belonged to the community, not to individuals. This does not mean that native standards are softer, rather they are different.

Native communities have often acted sternly against wrongdoers when the need arose. Under native tradition banishment from the community was not an unusual punishment. The Canadian system has not always upheld banishment as a recognized punishment. When a judge in northern Saskatchewan imposed an order banishing a thief from his home community for one year the order was overturned by the Saskatchewan Court of Appeal. Other courts have, however, upheld banishment orders.

The conflict between the Canadian legal system and native values is most evident in the area of child welfare. In all Canadian jurisdictions children who are abandoned or in need of protection can be apprehended and taken into state protection. There have been numerous instances of native children being seized because they were not in the care of their parents, but in the proper care of grandparents, uncles, aunts or other relatives. In most native communities the family means not only parents but also grandparents and other immediate relatives, and it is the family, not only the parents, who are responsible for the upbringing of children. To further complicate matters, when native children were and often still are apprehended, more often than not they are placed in white foster homes rather than in a home of the extended family. (Canadian child welfare authorities have even given native children for adoption in the United States.) Such practices are gradually changing as a result of growing concern by native communities. More and more native communities are taking control over such areas as child welfare. The Spallumcheen Indian band in B.C. was the first Indian group to taken action in this area. In 1980, in a unilateral move to which federal and provincial governments later agreed, the band passed a child welfare law. Under that law the priority of placement of children in need of protection was first with the extended family on the reserve, then with extended family on another reserve, then with extended family off reserve and only as a last resort were children to be placed in an non-Indian family.

It is because of such concerns as these that native communities speak of the need for self-government and the power to make and enforce their own laws, but there are still many problems and questions which have to be resolved before Indian government can become reality.

First and foremost is the issue of how much power these governments should have. Should native governments be able to make their own criminal laws or should their citizens be subject to the Criminal Code of Canada, as are all other Canadians? Should they have their own rules for divorce or should they be subject to the federal Divorce Act as are all other Canadians? Some native organizations have suggested that native governments should have powers to make criminal laws and deal with social questions such as divorce. They argue that such powers are necessary to ensure that native traditions and customs are reflected in those laws. The question is whether other Canadians would be prepared to accept differing standards for the law they have to answer to and the law that citizens of native governments have to answer to.

Another area of crucial importance to native people has been wildlife. Hunting, fishing and trapping are still an important means of livelihood for many native people. Hunting game can also be an important facet of native religion. For example, according to the beliefs of the West Coast Salish Indians it is necessary to hunt and burn fresh flesh to satisfy the hunger of one's deceased ancestors. Such practices often run afoul of provincial legislation — two Salish Indians were convicted of infringing provincial game laws and their conviction was upheld by the Supreme Court of Canada in 1985. For these reasons, native leaders argue that it is essential that native governments have the control and management of wild game. They argue that they are far more likely to effectively implement game conservation practices than any provincial government.

Another major issue is how native governments would be financed. Would they be entirely dependent on grants from federal and provincial governments or is it realistic to expect that they could finance themselves from their own tax base? Certainly the current financial position of many native communities could not provide an economic base to support government institutions.

The issue of cost is a major concern, and probably one reason why some provinces are afraid of self-government. The argument has been made that additional costs will be minimal because in large part the resources currently spent on Indians will simply be transferred to Indians. However, as is evident from the social conditions in most native communities the monies currently spent on native programming are less than adequate. The extent of the cost will not be known until the governments are in place. Costs will be dependent on the powers native governments are allowed to exercise. While land claim settlements and granting of further resource bases will help finance native governments, it is clear that at least in the short run, transfer payments from senior governments will have to be made to ensure the financial viability of native governments. It is also the cost factor that will probably force many native communities to form regional governments in order to achieve some degree of operational efficiency.

Questions also arise as to whether the native government would have jurisdiction over non-natives who happen to be on native government territory, or over native people outside native territory. For example, an Indian child is found in Edmonton, neglected by its parents. The parents and child are originally from the Our Land Indian Reserve, located approximately 200 kilometres northeast of Edmonton. The band has a fully operational Indian government that has passed laws and put in place the administrative machinery necessary for an operational child welfare system. Should the Indian government of Our Land have any say in this case? Should Edmonton authorities turn the case over to the Our Land people? Or should the Our Land system be restricted to Our Land Reserve? It should be remembered that a significant percentage, estimated to be 30 per cent and still increasing, of Canada's native population resides in urban centres. The argument against Indian governments having jurisdiction over these people is that by moving to the city these people may conciously intend to remove themselves from the jurisdiction of the Indian government. On the other hand native governments might be in a far better position to deal with native urban issues.

A corollary problem arises: should there be separate native governmental institutions in urban centres where there is a significant native population. Should there be, for example, separate Indian school boards? This is not a radical concept in view of the fact that separate school systems (with public funding) operate in a number of provinces. Similarly, should there be a separate native child welfare system to handle urban native child welfare?

Similar questions arise regarding the Métis. Currently they do not have a land base, which raises the question of whether you can have a government without there being some territory over which the government can rule.

The most likely scenario for southern Canada (a different situation exists in the north, which will be discussed later in the chapter) is that there will be native governments on Indian reserves and in Métis settlements, which will have jurisdiction over everyone within the geographic area covered by the government. Because of the fact that outside Alberta there are almost no lands set aside for Métis, their self-government is still in the distant future. Indian governments will probably not have the same powers as provinces, but in areas dealing with culture they are likely to have more power than provinces. There will be no jurisdiction beyond reserve boundaries. However, in some urban centres it is conceivable that there may be native school boards and child welfare systems. Similarly, arrangements are conceivable wherein natives sentenced in urban centres could serve their sentence in their home communities.

The scenario of hundreds of little provinces stretched across Canada has been painted by many critics of Indian self-government. An Ottawa writer, Ben Malkin, writing in various newpapers on the recommendations of the Special Parliamentary Committee on Indian Self-government stated: "...But it would be a provincial government based on the abhorrent apartheid principle of ethnic jurisdiction...Besides an abhorrent principle, there is the practical problem of creating some 300 new provinces — there are approximately that many Indian bands [there are in fact 550] — each with its own bureaucracy, each with its own confrontational issues to place before a federal government already sufficiently bemused by the demands of only 10 provinces." Another columnist, Don McGillivray, wrote: "...A serious matter such as the establishment of postage-stamp provinces here and there on a racially segregated basis should be honestly debated. Indians deserve better than apartheid..." Such critics ignore several points. Indian self-government is not apartheid. Apartheid is a policy of forced racial segregation. Indian self-government is a voluntary joining together of Indian peoples to run their own affairs. That is self-determination. No one is suggesting that Indians (or natives) will have to move back to their reserve and be subject to the rule of the reserve government. The decision to become a part of an Indian community will be voluntary. Ethnically-based governments are not a novelty in Canada. The province of Quebec, for example, protects the French fact in Canada.

Nor are there likely to be hundreds of postage-stamp-size provinces. Because many Indian reserves are geographically small and have a small economic and population base, the great majority do not have, and in all likelihood never will have, the capacity to offer a full range of government services. In reality, they will have to join together in regional governments (perhaps covering all the reserves in a province or even in a region) in order to be able to offer the full range of services. Conceivably all Indian bands might unite to form one Indian government for all of Canada. In many cases Indian (or Métis) governments will decide to contract with existing agencies to provide services. Thus, it is possible that police, health, educational and other services on reserves will be provided by existing agencies. This is not an uncommon feature on the Canadian scene. The most common example is policing — police services in a number of provinces are provided under contract by the RCMP, a federal force.

Steps Already Taken Towards Self-Government

Indian self-government has moved beyond the discussion stage. Various concrete steps have been and are being taken in that direction. It is very likely that by the year 2000 the great majority of Canada's native people will have at least some degree of self-government.

In recent years, some Indian bands have begun setting up governmental structures regardless of what the Indian Act or federal bureaucrats say about the situation. Such unilateral action has certainly acted as a stimulus for the federal government to move.

Canadian legislation has always allowed Indian bands to have some say in running their affairs (albeit a very limited one — sometimes it has been nothing more than the right to elect a chief and council, who could be thrown out of office by the Indian Affairs bureaucracy). Generally, early Canadian Indian Act legislation provided for an elected system of chief and council (displacing traditional methods of selecting leaders) and vested limited bylaw-making power in them. Such powers could, however, be overridden by the Indian agent or other officials of the Indian bureaucracy.

There was a major rewriting of the Indian Act in 1951. Band councils were given further bylaw-making powers, including authority over such diverse subjects as regulation of traffic, control of noxious weeds, regulation of bee-keeping, control over door-to-door salespeople, some power to regulate construction work on reserves, keeping law and order on reserves and other similar matters. However, any bylaw passed could be disallowed by the minister of Indian affairs. Also in 1951, a provision was introduced, whereby if the government felt that an Indian band had reached "an advanced stage of development" the band could be allowed to raise money by taxation and exercise other financial powers. Such powers could be unilaterally withdrawn from a band at any time.

The 1970s and '80s have seen a gradual transfer of some of the powers exercised by the Indian Affairs Department to band councils and regional Indian organizations. Indian Affairs runs education, health, economic development, welfare and other programs on reserves. In 1971 some 16 per cent of the budget for such services was administered by Indian bands or organizations; by the 1982/83 fiscal year that had increased to 50 per cent. Thus while there has been a devolution of administration, this is still not self-government. Program priorities, design and reporting are set by Indian Affairs. Self-government means setting your own priorities and designing your own programs. Such a transfer of administration does help train and create the Indian governmental structures that will be needed for functioning governments.

In 1985 federal Indian Affairs Minister Crombie announced a plan to enter into bilateral negotiations with individual Indian bands to allow them to govern their own affairs. The 650-member Sechelt Indian Band in B.C. was the first to benefit from the plan. The federal government can, under its constitutional responsibility, proceed unilaterally in creating Indian governments. Self-government is also on the way in Ontario. In December of 1985 the federal government, the Ontario government and various Ontario Indian groups (including the Union of Ontario Indians, Association of Iroquois and Allied Indians, Nishnawbe Aski Nation and the Grand Council of Treaty Three) signed a declaration of political intent to negotiate the establishment of Indian self-government in Ontario.

These recent events amount to a devolution of power, wherein Ottawa will give up the administration of some of its programs to Indian bands. This is not yet self-government, but it is a definite move in that direction; Indian administration of programs is replacing Ottawa-administered programs. Whether this devolution of power will lead to self-government in its true sense remains to be seen.

Self-Government in the North

It is in the Northwest Territories that the greatest progress has been made towards self-government. The Territories cover over 3.4 million square kilometres (one-third of Canada) but have a population of slightly less than 50,000. Close to 60 per cent of the population is native, including approximately 17,000 Inuit. Discussions are now under way to split the territory into a western and eastern half. The eastern half would become Nunavut, the home of the Inuit. The western half would become Denendeh, home of the Dene Indians and the Métis.

A 1982 plebiscite over the split saw 56 per cent of the voters voting in favour. Late in 1982, then Indian Affairs Minister John Munro announced that the federal cabinet had agreed in principle to dividing the Northwest Territories. Several conditions were imposed by the federal government, including the settlement of native claims, agreement on the boundary between the two territories, the choosing of new capitals and definition of the distribution of powers between local, regional and territorial governments.

The Nunavut Constitutional Forum was formed in the summer of 1982 for the purpose of defining a government, through consultation with the people, for Nunavut. The Dene and Métis formed a similar body in the fall of 1982 known as the Western Constitutional Forum. These two groups in combination with the Legislative Assembly of the Northwest Territories have formed the Constitutional Alliance.

The most likely dividing line between the two states will be the tree line; with everything to the north and east being Nunavut. There have, however, been some areas of contention; the most notable being the western Arctic, which is inhabited by Inuvialuit people. These people culturally are tied to the Inuit of the eastern Arctic; however, many of their economic ties are with the western portion of the territories. There are also many resources in this area and undoubtedly both governments would like to see some revenue from such resources.

The Nunavut proposal can be summed up as follows: essentially the Inuit propose a provincial form of government, with a legislative assembly having the kinds of powers that southern legislatures possess. They do, however, propose that their government have some jurisdiction in foreign affairs. Primarily they want to ensure that they will be able to maintain contact with Inuit who live in other states, such as Greenland, Alaska, and the Soviet Union. This would be similar to the kind of arrangement that allows Quebec to participate in international forums related to franco-phone issues. Even today the Inuit, through the Inuit Circumpolar Conference, have active contact with Inuit in other nations, and they have participated in United Nations conferences on whaling. Inuktitut would be one of the official languages in Nunavut.

Denendeh would also become a kind of province under proposals developed by the Western Constitutional Forum. Denendeh would probably include a greater non-native population than Nunavut (Yellow-knife, which has a sizable non-native population, would probably fall within Denendeh). However, the proposals for Denendeh include various guarantees to ensure the survival of the Dene nation. Thus the Dene argue that Denendeh should have power over fisheries and navigable waters (currently areas of federal jurisdiction) to "ensure protection of the aquatic environment of Denendeh which is basic to our traditional Dene way of life" and also control over employment and labour in order to "preserve and develop historical Dene work styles and employment relations". The Charter of Founding Principles for Denendeh would include entrenchment of native languages as official languages. Many of the decisions in Denendeh would involve the whole community; with community assemblies making decisions by consensus and referendums held to ensure that decisions were widely based. To ensure the cultural and political survival of the Dene certain protections would be built into the constitution. Thus no matter what the Dene population was they would be guaranteed a minimum of 30 per cent of the seats on community councils and in the Legislative Assembly. Secondly, there would be a Dene Senate, composed entirely of Dene, which would have the power to veto any legislation which adversely affected aboriginal rights.

Of great concern to both the Dene and the Inuit is the possibility of a migration of southerners, who would take control of government institutions. It is for that reason that the Dene are asking for the constitutional guarantees that are set out above. The lesson of Manitoba has not been lost on native people of the north. Manitoba came into being as a Métis province, with guarantees of language and land rights. As has been seen, the Métis very quickly lost their rights, and many ended up leaving Manitoba. In the past the north has attracted many migrant southerners who have come to work on resource projects. Attracted by high wages, they usually keep a home base in southern Canada. In order to ensure that such people do not gain an inordinate amount of say in government both the Inuit and the Dene propose lengthy residence requirements for voting status. As a starting proposal, the Western Constitutional Forum recommended a ten-year residence requirement before one could vote while the Nunavut Constitutional Forum recommended a three-year requirement. Both groups feel that lengthy residence requirements will ensure that only true northerners will vote, but the fact that they would also effectively mean disenfranchisement for many has sparked considerable debate in southern Canada. Such provisions may even violate the Charter of Rights and Freedoms.

To the native people in the north the division of the Territories is a challenge, and they hope to avoid the mistakes made in southern Canada. In a 1984 brief to the House of Commons Standing Committee on Indian Affairs the Western Constitutional Forum described the challenge in the following way:

> First there is the challenge and opportunity for the Dene, the Métis and the Inuit to negotiate a relationship amongst themselves. Coupled with this is the challenge and the opportunity for the aboriginal groups and the non-native population to negotiate their relationship as well. It is an uncommon event in Canadian history for these parties to attempt to reach an agreement on how they can live and work together cooperatively without using the Federal Government as a mediator. Finally there is the challenge and the opportunity for the people of the north together to negotiate their relationship with the Government of Canada.

Discussions have also been under way in the Yukon, where a sizable portion of the population is Indian. Comprehensive land-claims-settlement discussions have been under way for a number of years. In fact, two tentative settlements, one in 1976 and the other in 1983, were reached but in the end were rejected by one side or the other. The 1983 settlement fell through when the federal government pulled out, saying it had waited too long for Yukon Indians to approve the tentative settlement and that there did not appear to be sufficient support amongst Yukon's 6,000 Indians for the tentative pact. The discussions included guarantees of control of internal affairs and special guaranteed participation in governmental affairs of direct interest to the Indians.

The James Bay and Northern Quebec Agreement also created Indian and Inuit governmental institutions. To a large extent, these institutions are similar to southern municipalities; however, in some areas they do have extensive control.

The American Experience

Lest the concept of Indian self-government seem radical it may be useful to look at the American experience. Indian self-governments have been functioning for over fifty years and have been supported by such conservative politicians as Richard Nixon and Ronald Reagan. Speaking to Congress in 1970 on Indian self-determination, Nixon said:

> Self-determination among the Indian people can and must be encouraged without the threat of eventual termination....We must assure the Indian that he can assume control of his own life without being separated involuntarily from the tribal group. And we must make it clear that Indians can become independent of federal control without being cut off from federal concern and federal support.

Thirteen years later Ronald Reagan spoke of sovereign Indian nations and of the Indian-United States relationship as that of "government to government".

In American law as early as the 1830s courts recognized Indian tribes as "dependent sovereign nations". In 1934 Congress gave official recognition to this legal theory with the passage of the Indian Reorganization Act. The focus of the act was to allow Indian tribes a measure of self-government on their reserves.

The powers of Indian governments in the United States are fairly wide. First, Indian tribes have the power to determine their own membership. Tribes have the power to draw up their own constitution (subject to certain restrictions) or they can choose to use model constitutions developed by the Bureau of Indian Affairs. They have full power to license and control businesses established on reserves and to raise revenue through taxation. They have extensive law-making powers; with the power to make laws dealing with divorce, wills, property ownership, traffic and some criminal matters. They have the power to establish their own court systems; indeed, tribal courts are a common feature on most U.S. Indian reserves. Procedures are set out for the appointment of judges (usually someone from the community — but not necessarily a lawyer), for the establishment of a bar (association of advocates or lawyers) and for appealing judgements. Tribal courts deal with a whole range of matters including criminal, family and civil cases.

There are however, several limitations on the powers of Indian governments in the United States. First, there is an Indian Civil Rights Act, passed by Congress in 1968, which is a code of individual rights that Indian governments and tribal courts must respect. The act requires that all persons subject to Indian governments must be granted equal protection by the law, must have the right to a lawyer if charged and cannot have their freedom of speech, the press or religion curtailed. Similarly, Congress in the act has restricted the sentencing power of tribal courts to a maximum of $500 and/or six months' imprisonment. (The act is the source of much criticism in some circles; some Indian leaders see it as the imposition of white standards on Indian governments). Congress has also defined fourteen major crimes (including murder) as being beyond the jurisdiction of Indian governments to prosecute or prescribe penalties for.

Indian governments in the United States are still dependent on the federal treasury for a significant part of their operating budgets. The Bureau of Indian Affairs still has an immense impact on Indian life. It still operates programs on some reserves and plays a supervisory role on most reserves. The social conditions that plague Canadian Indian communities — poverty, alcoholism, unemployment — are equally prevalent on many Indian reserves in the United States.

Some Questions to be Resolved

The message to be drawn from the American experience is that native self-government will not solve all problems. There is a need to see Indian governments in realistic terms. Simply turning over management to natives will not end poverty. True self-determination requires an economic base, which in turn requires the resolution of land claims. Perhaps the aboriginal people should be looked upon as landlords who are allowing their land to be leased for development. In return for the lease they will get regular rental payments, which will in turn support native governments and native development.

Both native and Canadian governments will have to deal with the issue of the extent of development that should be allowed on Indian lands. Should there be lands left undeveloped for those native people who wish to continue to live off the land? In other words, is the industrial model of society the one that should be imposed on Indian lands?

Once it is implemented there will of course be other problems created by Indian government. In the United States there has been considerable litigation, defining where the authority of tribal governments ends. There have been disputes about jurisdiction over non-Indians doing business on the reserve, and about the extent of the powers of tribal courts. In fact, there is a whole subcategory of the legal system devoted to such questions.

There will also be those Indian people who from time to time will be unhappy with the actions of their government. These potential problems raise the question of the extent to which non-Indian institutions should be involved in such issues. For example, if an accused complains that he was sentenced to jail by a tribal court without having the right to a lawyer (in some U.S. tribal courts attorneys are discouraged or banned). Should he be able to come to superior provincial court asking for an order that his conviction be overturned? Should he be able to argue that the Charter of Rights applies to the Indian court? Should a citizen of an Indian government have the right to have the election of a chief turned aside for corruption, even though the Indian court has refused to do so? Should there be recourse for the business person who has been refused a trading licence? In essence, the problem comes down to this: whether Canadian society will allow Indian nations full control of their affairs, or insist on minimum standards being met by the governments. These are all problems that have been grappled with in the United States. By and large, the American answer has been to impose a system of rules and standards within which Indian governments must operate. This has not always been a happy compromise as many Indian leaders feel they are severely hampered by big government watching over them.

The American experience also shows the necessity for Indian governments to evolve over a period of time. It would be wrong to impose a model and leave no room for it to grow and change to accommodate some of the problems discussed above.

What Canada Must Do

If there is a sad chapter in Canadian history it certainly has to be the story of relations with the native community. Canada now has an unprecedented opportunity to learn from the past and set out in new directions. Native people must be given the opportunity to manage their own affairs and they must be ensured sufficient resources to do the job adequately. In many respects, Canada has been a world leader in the last decade in dealing with aboriginal issues, but there is still much to do. By establishing effective self-government models Canada can set a standard for other nations with indigenous populations.

Domestically, the federal government in co-operation with the provinces needs to sit down and seriously evaluate past policies with a view to correcting earlier mistakes. While Indians, Inuit and perhaps Métis are constitutionally a federal responsibility, the reality of Canada is that the provinces need to be involved if Canada is to have a meaningful national policy on native rights. If self-government is to work, provincial co-operation is needed.

Canada also has a duty, in view of its sizable indigenous population, to speak out at international forums on the treatment of aboriginal peoples in other parts

of the world. A starting-point would be to press for
international standards for the treatment of indigenous
peoples. International pressure is being brought to bear
on South Africa to change its apartheid policies. What
is happening to aboriginal peoples in many countries
is as bad or worse than what apartheid is doing to
blacks in South Africa. Surely there is a need for the
same type of concerted international lobbying to protect
aboriginal peoples.

Selected Bibliography

Books

Asch, Michael. *Home and Native Land, Aboriginal Rights and the Canadian Constitution*. Toronto: Methuen, 1984

Berton, Pierre. *The Promised Land, Settling the West 1896-1914*. Toronto: McClelland and Stewart, 1984

Boldt, Menno and Long, J. Anthony, ed. *The Quest for Justice*. Toronto: University of Toronto Press, 1985

Brown, Dee. *Bury My Heart at Wounded Knee*. Holt, Rinehart & Winston, 1970

Cardinal, Harold. *The Unjust Society: the Tragedy of Canada's Indians*. Edmonton: M.G. Hurtig, 1969

Cumming, Peter A., and Mickenberg, Neil H. *Native Rights in Canada*(2nd ed.). Toronto: General Publishing, 1972

Daniels, Harry W. ed. *The Forgotten People, Metis and non-status Indian Land Claims*. Ottawa: Native Council of Canada, 1979

Dobbin, Murray. *The One-and-a-Half Men*. Vancouver: New Star Books, 1981

Frideres, James S. *Native People in Canada, Contemporary Conflicts* (2nd ed.). Scarborough: Prentice-Hall Canada, 1983

Friesen, Gerald. *The Canadian Prairies, A History*. Toronto: University of Toronto Press, 1984

Fumoleau, René. *As Long As This Land Shall Last*. Toronto: McClelland & Stewart, 1977

Getty, Ian A.L. and Lussier, Antoine S., ed. *As Long as the Sun Shines and Water Flows, A Reader in Canadian Native Studies*. Vancouver: University of British Columbia Press, 1983

Harper, Vern. *Following the Red Path, The Native People's Caravan, 1974*. Toronto: NC Press, 1979

Hurley, J.D. *Children or Brethren: Aboriginal Rights in Colonial Iroquoia*. Saskatoon: University of Saskatchewan Native Law Centre, 1986

Indian Law Resource Centre. *Indian Rights Human Rights, Handbook for Indians on International Human Rights Complaints Procedures*. Washington: Indian Law Resource Centre, 1984

Jenness, Diamond. *Indians of Canada* (7th ed.). Toronto: University of Toronto Press, 1977

Kane, Paul. *Wanderings of an Artist Among the Indians of North America*. Edmonton: M.G. Hurtig, 1968

Metis Association of Alberta, Joe Sawchuk, Patricia Sawchuk and Theresa Ferguson. *Metis Land Rights in Alberta: A Political History*. Edmonton: Metis Association of Alberta, 1981

Morris, Alexander. *The Treaties of Canada with the Indians*. Toronto: P.R. Randall, 1862; fascimile ed. Toronto: Coles Publishing Co., 1979

Price, John. *Indians of Canada*. Scarborough: Prentice-Hall of Canada, 1979

Morse, Bradford W. ed. *Aboriginal Peoples and the Law, Indian, Metis and Inuit Rights in Canada*. Ottawa: Carleton University Press, 1985

Raunet, Daniel. *Without Surrender, Without Consent, A History of the Nishga Land Claims*. Vancouver: Douglas & McIntyre, 1984

Richardson, Boyce. *Strangers Devour the Land*. Toronto: MacMillan, 1975

Sawchuk, Joe. *The Metis of Manitoba, Reformulation of an Ethnic Identity*. Toronto: Peter Martin Associates, 1978

Slattery, Brian. *The Land Rights of Indigenous Canadian Peoples*. Saskatoon: University of Saskatchewan Native Law Centre, 1979

Weaver, Sally M.. *Making Canadian Indian Policy, The Hidden Agenda 1968-1970*. Toronto: University of Toronto Press, 1981

Government Reports

Alaska Highway Pipeline Inquiry. Minister of Supply and Services, Canada, 1977

House of Commons. *Indian Self-Government in Canada, Report of the Special Committee*. Canada, 1983

Task Force to Review Comprehensive Claims Policy 1985. *Living Treaties: Lasting Agreements, Report of the Task Force to Review Comprehensive Claims Policy*. Department of Indian Affairs and Northern Development, Ottawa, 1985

Treaties and Historical Research Centre, P.R.E. Group. *The Historical Development of the Indian Act*. Department of Indian and Northern Affairs, Ottawa, 1978

The Report of the Mackenzie Valley Pipeline Inquiry. Minister of Supply and Services, Canada, 1977

Report of the MacEwan Joint Metis-Government Committee to Review the Metis Betterment Act and Regulations. Alberta Department of Municipal Affairs, Edmonton, 1984

Articles, Monographs and Non-government reports

Bartlett, Richard H.. *Indian Reserves in Atlantic Canada*. Saskatoon: University of Saskatchewan Native Law Centre, 1986

Bartlett, Richard H. "Indian Reserves on the Prairies." (1985) 23 Alberta Law Review (No. 2) 243

Bartlett, Richard H.. *Indian Reserves in Quebec*. Saskatoon: University of Saskatchewan Native Law Centre, 1984

Bartlett, Richard H.. *The Indian Act of Canada*. Saskatoon: University of Saskatchewan Native Law Centre, 1980

Crawford, John C. "Speaking Michif in Four Metis Communities." (1983) 3 Canadian Journal of Native Studies 47

Little Bear, Leroy. "A Concept of Native Title." (1982) 5 Canadian Legal Aid Bulletin (Part II) 99

McNeil, Kent. *Native Rights and the Boundaries of Rupert's Land and the North-Western Territory*. Saskatoon: University of Saskatchewan Native Law Centre, 1982

Morse, Bradford W. "The Original Peoples of Canada, "(1982) Canadian Legal Aid Bulletin (Part I) 1

Sprague, D.N. "Government Lawlessness in the Administration of Manitoba Land Claims, 1870-1887." (1980) 10 Manitoba Law Journal 415

Zlotkin, Norman K.. *Unfinished Business, Aboriginal Peoples and the 1983 Constitutional Conference*. Institute of Intergovernmental Affairs, Queen's University, 1983

Zlotkin, Norman K. "The 1983 and 1984 Constitutional Conferences: Only the Beginning." (1984) 3 Canadian Native Law Reporter 3

Western Constitutional Forum. *Partners for the Future, A Selection of Papers Related to Constitutional Development in the Western Northwest Territories*. Yellowknife, 1985

INDEX

244 Index

231-235; Native self-government, 231-233; Race riots, 188
United States Indian Claims Commission, 51
United States Supreme Court, 48
Upper Canada, Indian affairs, 70, 124, 139. *See also* Ontario
Upper Fort Garry, 160

Vancouver Island, 144
Vitoria, Francisco de, 41-43
Viva, Father Francisco, 27

Walpole Island Reserve, 215
War of 1812, 113
West, Alienation, 172, 189; settlement, 79
Western Constitutional Forum, 227-230

"Whiskey Forts," 78
White Bear Reserve, 151
White Paper on Indian Policy, 1969, 33, 142, 183, 184, 186, 187, 190, 213, 214
Whitehorse, Yukon Territory, 90
Williams (Indian), 111
Wills, 128
Winnipeg River, 13
Worcester's Case, 49
World Council of Indigenous Peoples, Ottawa, 43, 206
"World reversal," 12, 29, 81
Wounded Knee, South Dakota, Massacre, 1890, 82

Yanomami Indians, Brazil, 43
Yucatan Peninsula, 41
Yukon gold rush, 89
Yukon Territory, 90

Other Books in the Canadian Issues Series

Misguided Missiles
Canada, the Cruise and Star Wars
SIMON ROSENBLUM

Canada is divided over whether to participate in the development of the Cruise Missile and "Star Wars". Simon Rosenblum argues that Canadian involvement in these and other elements of the U.S. nuclear strategy is drawing the country into Pentagon plans for nuclear "first strikes" and "limited nuclear war."

"It provides valuable insights for a more well-informed, soundly reasoned debate on Canada's role in the arms race." — *Now*, Toronto.

Canada's Colonies
A History of the Yukon and Northwest Territories
KENNETH COATES

The history of the North has received little attention — in part because of the slight status of "Canada's Colonies" in the national scheme of things, and in part because of powerful romantic images of explorers and gold miners that have governed the Canadian concept of this region. Kenneth Coate's book relates history as seen from the North, from the vibrant pre-contact cultures of the Inuit and Dene to the land claim, resource project and self-government controversies of the 1980s.

Police
Urban Policing in Canada

JOHN SEWELL

This informative primer by Canada's best-known urban reformer, John Sewell, fills the information vacuum that reduces most discussion of policing to "for" or "against." The book begins with an outline history of policing and a discussion of the "true" extent of crime. Sewell then turns to the day-to-day issues of policing, from the effectiveness of patrol work to the drawbacks of rigid police hierarchies.

"A handy elementary guide to the basics of policing today." — *Montreal Gazette*.

The West
The History of a Region in Confederation

J.F. CONWAY

Since settlers first tried to eke out a living on the banks of the Red River, Western Canadians have felt that the West's place in the Canadian scheme of things is a subordinate one. John Conway's book is a history of Confederation from the point of view of the four western provinces. Conway shows that although the focus of western dissatisfaction may have changed in recent years, the root cause of having to "buy dear and sell cheap" remains.

"A must for anyone who wishes to know about the recent economic and political past of Western Canada." — *Lethbridge Herald*

Ethics and Economics
Canada's Catholic Bishops on the Economic Crisis
GREGORY BAUM AND DUNCAN CAMERON

The most talked-about political manifesto of recent years is "Ethical Reflections on the Economic Crisis," issued in early 1983 by Canada's Catholic bishops. The statement's impact reverberated through political, church and business circles because of its trenchant critique of the structural problems of Canadian society and the economy.

This book takes the issues raised by the bishops several steps further. "Ethical Reflections" is included, followed by two wide-ranging commentaries: one from an ethical point of view, by Gregory Baum; the other from an economic perspective, by Duncan Cameron. Several earlier statements by the bishops are also included as a guide to further reading on this subject.

"A major contribution to the understanding of the Canadian Church." — *Catholic New Times*

Oil and Gas
Ottawa, the Provinces and the Petroleum Industry
JAMES LAXER

For more than a decade, the oil industry and energy policy have been a central issue in Canadian economic and political life. *Oil and Gas* offers an overview of these turbulent years and fresh insight into the motives of the main players: Ottawa, Alberta and other producing provinces, the oil majors such as Imperial, the Canadian companies like Petro-Canada, the OPEC cartel and the U.S. government.

"Provocative reading" — *Canadian Public Policy*

Women and Work
Inequality in the Labour Market
PAUL PHILLIPS AND ERIN PHILLIPS

Why are women still second-class citizens at work? To answer this question, Paul and Erin Phillips trace women's involvement in the paid labour market, and in labour unions, throughout Canadian history. They document the disadvantages that women face today and examine the explanations that have been forwarded for the persistence of these problems. Chapters are devoted to the effect of technological changes such as the microelectronic "chip" on women's work and to proposals for bringing about equality in the labour market.

"A fine salute to the strong body of materials on women's work that has sprung into being in the last decade." — *Toronto Star*

The New Canadian Constitution
DAVID MILNE

The New Canadian Constitution explains just what everyone wanted out of the constitution-making process, who got what, and what the final results mean for Canadians. Of special interest is the concluding chapter, which examines the nature of the new constitution in terms of interests, issues and accidents that shaped it, and its own strengths and weaknesses.

"...a straightforward and comprehensive narrative." — *Globe and Mail*